SOUTH FROM SAN FRANCISCO came the

Society of Civil Engineers in 1896, to view a landmark in

engineering progress: the new Crystal Springs Dam.

Today, in 1963, the increasing waters that flow from this dam,

symbolic of the silent, intensifying growth of almost

everything on this Peninsula, are piped into 21 cities in

three counties, to reach the homes of 1,500,000 people.

Crystal Springs Dam — a Landmark and a Symbol.

# SOUTH
# FROM SAN FRANCISCO

## San Mateo County, California

*Its History and Heritage*

By Frank M. Stanger

PUBLISHED BY THE

SAN MATEO COUNTY HISTORICAL ASSOCIATION

MCMLXIII

*Library of Congress Catalog Card No. 63-21262*

Linotype Composition: Times Printing, San Mateo
Lithographed by Peninsula Lithograph Co.

# Foreword

South from the Golden Gate lies San Francisco, and beyond it the County of San Mateo. Together they cover the Peninsula—or at least most of it.

"The Peninsula" (for the benefit of our many strangers and newcomers) is a number of things. It is a forty-mile strip of land that separates San Francisco Bay from the Pacific Ocean; it is also a string of rugged hills, some of which aspire to the level of mountains, reaching from northern fog to southern sunny slopes, with intervening wooded canyons and scraggy seashore. And this is only the beginning of a definition.

One finds it easy to become sentimental about country like this. People here say "it has everything," and we confess, perhaps with some prejudice, that we are inclined to agree.

But history has not divided this charmed area in equal portions. The world-famous City-and-County of San Francisco manages to live within a compact 45 square miles, and in population seems to have reached a saturation point at about three-quarters of a million people. The County of San Mateo, on the other hand, with 454 square miles, is believed to have just passed the half-a-million mark, and each new day brings something like 57 more inhabitants—a total of more than 20,000 every year.

San Mateo County's history is, of course, intertwined with that of San Francisco and the rest of the Bay Area; and what is more, due to its position at the great crossroads of the West (the Bay and its Golden Gateway to the interior), it has always been very much a part of California and in the forefront of all new developments.

The Peninsula's story starts with the discovery of a people who were among the most primitive of Stone-Age Indians; it becomes involved successively with two frontiers—one Spanish and the other Anglo-American, and it carries us, finally, deep into the swirl of today's complex and seething urban culture. Probably no one picture of human history could possibly encompass a wider range of social patterns and levels of living. Yet it all happened right here.

This book, however, makes no pretense of being a treatise on comparative cultures. It is designed rather as a source of home-town information, primarily for the more-than-a-million people who now live south of the Golden Gate, sharing the limited space between the Bay and the Ocean.

We who live here, whether we realize it or not, and whether we were born here or arrived only yesterday, are now a part of this history; we are, willy-nilly, the actors now on stage in an ever on-going drama. Let us hope that, with some awareness of what has gone before, we may be inspired to put on a worthy performance for our generation.

# Acknowledgments

The publishing of this book is a bold venture, for our County Historical Association, made possible only by the fact that certain of our most able and busy citizens have been willing to give their time and energy to the undertaking.

That we normally count on the guidance of capable and history-minded citizens from all parts of the County, is obvious from the roster of our Board of Directors: Our President, J. Hart Clinton, lives in San Mateo, as do also Miss Winifred Burke, Recording Secretary Francis Guido, George N. Keyston, and Dr. Harold F. Taggart. Our Vice President, Mrs. David D. Bohannon, and Mrs. Ralph K. Davies, live in Woodside; the Treasurer, Paul A. McCarthy, together with John E. Newman and Mrs. Ray Spangler, hail from Redwood City; F. A. Ammerman lives in Burlingame, Miss Rue Clifford in South San Francisco, Mrs. P. H. Evarts in Millbrae, Mrs. A. S. Kalenborn in San Carlos, Miss Irene Simpson in Hillsborough, and Mrs. Frank Williamson in Pescadero.

But this task has required more than guidance. Besides the Board's having shouldered the responsibility for the volume, and certain individuals having generously underwritten any financial risk, preparation of the book has involved an enormous amount of volunteer work.

The organizing and directing of this entire effort has been ably done by Mr. George N. Keyston, retired business man, and his special committee consisting of Miss Mary Ellen Mulhall, of the College of San Mateo faculty; Miss Irene Simpson, Director of Wells Fargo History Room in San Francisco; and Dr. Harold F. Taggart, Emeritus Dean of the College of San Mateo.

Mr. Keyston in particular has given almost his entire time to the project; first, in exploring publication methods; then in securing donations of professional assistance and material; and lastly, in triggering a pre-publication sales campaign so effectively that the financial success of the venture was assured before the book was off the press.

The nine members of our regular Women's Auxiliary have shared in the effort whenever and however needed. Mrs. Earl F. Schmidt and Mrs. Theodore M. Holmes served successively as Chairman. The other members are Mrs. Paul T. Beale, Mrs. Geoffrey W. Bromfield, Mrs. Ralph W. Gaines, Mrs. Frank J. Losey, Mrs. John C. Meyer, Mrs. Paul D. Steiner and Mrs. Harry W. Tracy. Their most noteworthy contribution was in the preparation and mailing of some thousands of letters. Miss Grace McAuliffe has assisted as proofreader, and Miss Mary Ellen Mulhall has donated her professional skill and know-how to visualizing the design and executing the layout, assisted in busy moments by Misses Anne Wickland and Patricia Toohig. All told, this book is the product of a large cooperative effort.

F. M. Stanger.

# Table of Contents

# I. Discovery: *The Bay, the Land, the People*

*"Let our students survey the history of all mankind all over the face of the planet since the age when man's pre-human ancestors first became human; but at the same time let them scrutinize the history of some local short-lived tribe or parish."*                     ARNOLD TOYNBEE

Father Juan Crespi was chaplain and diarist for a party of Spanish explorers who, as explorers, were not doing very well. Under orders from no less an authority than a direct emissary of King Carlos III of Spain, they were searching for the harbor of Monterey, preparatory to founding a settlement there; but instead of finding it, they were beginning to wonder if they themselves were not lost.

But on November 2, 1769, Crespi's recording of routine events was broken by news that seemed important. Some of the men in the party, who had been deer hunting, reported that from a hilltop they had seen to the northward "an immense arm of the sea or an estuary which penetrated into the land as far as the eye could reach, extending to the southeast; that they had seen some beautiful plains well adorned with trees, and that the smokes which they saw in all directions left no doubt that the country was thickly populated with heathen villages."

This news was in fact much more important than Crespi even dreamed—it was the world's first recorded hint of the existence of San Francisco Bay, and the "beautiful plains well adorned with trees" were the sun-lit slopes of San Mateo County that border it.

Today's lovers of the Bay Area will expect, at this point, to read that the news caused great excitement in camp, but not so; and the small stir that it did produce had nothing whatever to do with the discovery of a great bay. A new harbor would not cure the scurvy, nor would it bring this bewildered party any nearer to Monterey Bay, the harbor that they must find.

Unless—and to these hungry and travel-weary men this was the only interesting thing about the hunters' report—unless this new "estuary" might possibly be Monterey.

These events, so oddly confused, took place in a camp that was nowhere near Monterey. The site is now in the city of Pacifica, San Mateo County—close to the ocean shore in the sheltered and beautiful Pedro Valley. Here for two days a band

1

of explorers, under the command of Captain Gaspar de Portolá, Governor of The Californias, had been resting uneasily and refreshing themselves, as they could, on the mussels they had found at San Pedro Point. They were waiting for their scout, Sgt. José Francisco Ortega, to return from an important reconnoitering trip northward.

His urgent mission was to find the answer to their great and baffling question: was the elusive Bay of Monterey still ahead of them, or had they somehow passed it by? Tomorrow he should return, and surely he would bring an answer that would be vital to the success of their long trip from San Diego—perhaps even to their own survival.

The next night, when the firing of guns announced Ortega's coming, all hands rushed out to meet him. What had he found? There was indeed a water barrier ahead, and he undoubtedly had seen the great estuary that "extended to the southeast" (though the record makes no mention of it); but the big news, so big that it crowded everything else out, was what the Indians had told him, or so he thought. Two days' journey northward, beyond this water barrier, they said, there was a bay with a ship in it.

This was greater news than they had even hoped for—so good that even the possibility of Ortega's having misinterpreted the sign language did not dampen their eagerness. It could only mean that the bay farther north was their long-sought Monterey, and that a ship from San Diego was waiting there with supplies and relief for them. With this new prospect, their next move became obvious to everyone: they must try at all hazards to get around this large estuary, or whatever it might be, and reach that other bay.

So it was that the next day, November 4, 1769, the entire party, as Crespi tells it, "set out to continue the journey, following the beach to the north. We then entered the mountains, directing our course to the northeast and from the summit of a peak beheld the great estuary."

This so-called peak is a part of the Peninsula's Sweeney Ridge, only slightly higher than the ridge itself. From it one now looks down on the cities of Millbrae and San Bruno, or westward on the city of Pacifica. Near it, in these years of the 1960's, is a marker of sorts—the army's radar dome that can be seen from both the Bayside and the Coastside. From this point Portolá and his entire party got their first view of the great Bay of San Francisco.

But at that time they could not sense the importance to the civilized world of what they saw. Months later, with the perspective of afterthought, Crespi gathered enthusiasm enough to describe it as a great harbor that "could shelter not only the King's navy but all the navies of Europe." But just now its very bigness was depressing; it was a barrier between them and what they believed was relief from their short rations and from many more weeks of travel.

They descended the steep eastern slope of the ridge, heading southward, and camped for the night. It was journey enough for one day, just to get over this ridge —for the able-bodied men as well as for the scurvy victims who were carried on improvised stretchers slung between two mules. Their camp site is now beneath the waters of San Andreas Lake; a sign on the Skyline Boulevard points to it.

San Pedro Valley, showing Sweeney Ridge upper right, where
Portolá first viewed San Francisco Bay. Below: Point San Pedro.

The next day took them some ten miles farther southward. Traveling in their accustomed order, out in front rode the scout, Sergeant Ortega. He, as usual, had already pioneered the day's trek and selected the next night's camp site. At the head of the main party came the Commander, Captain Portolá, followed by other officers and the two Franciscan friars, Fathers Crespi and Francisco Gómez. With them were Lieut. Pedro Fages and the capable young army engineer, Miguel de Costansó, who also kept a journal. He and Crespi seem to have collaborated rather closely—in fact, comparing the two accounts, one often wonders who copied whom!

Next came a squad of Catalonian soldiers, some Indians from Lower California, the engineer corps, and the pack train. Finally, there was the rear guard, commanded by Captain Fernando Rivera. What with servants and muleteers, a party of some sixty men with two hundred horses and mules crawled slowly over the dry autumn hills and down the brushy ravines, following the valley that is now filled with the Crystal Springs Lakes. The unmarked site of the next camp was somewhere near the southerly end of those lakes.

The following day, still moving to get around the great "estuary," which was the south portion of San Francisco Bay, they continued down the route of today's Cañada Road, until they observed that the hills ahead of them would bar their further progress in that direction. At the same time, the hills on their left came to an end, hence they swung toward the east; but the language of the journals leaves us uncertain whether this turn was made near the present site of Searsville Lake, or at the end of the valley that now bears the name of Portolá—except that American usage has changed it to Portóla.

But the site of their next history-making camp is well established. It was on San Francisquito Creek at the spot where *El Camino Real* and the railroad cross it, entering the city of Palo Alto. At this point stands the tall redwood tree (the *"palo alto,"* which means tall tree) that has given its name to a famous city. A marker under this tree tells the story.

Realizing that they were now near the south end of the Bay, the order was again issued that the tired expedition should rest while the ever-active Ortega and his scouts probed the unknown country of the East Bay.

The scouts took their allotted time of four days but, on their return, gloom again settled over the camp. The distance was great; they had found their progress challenged by hostile Indians; and the land was burned over, leaving no pasture for their animals. But they had gone far enough, probably to the hills east of Berkeley or Richmond, to get a view of "another immense estuary" which extended inland. This was San Pablo Bay and, perhaps, Suisun Bay. Furthermore, Ortega had decided, on chilling second thought, that the supposed ship in a distant bay was all a mistake, born more likely of his own wishful thinking than of any vague signs that the Indians made.

It may not have been entirely a figment of his imagination. Among the Indians along the coast there undoubtedly were legends that stemmed from the visits of Cermenho, who sailed for Spain but was shipwrecked at Point Reyes, and Francis Drake, the British "pirate" who had landed and parlayed with the Indians, supposedly at Drake's Bay, both of them nearly two centuries earlier. It could well have been this story that the Costaño Indians were now trying to communicate to the new strangers.

After a council meeting in the Captain's tent, the decision was made to accept the verdict of failure—failure, that is, to find Monterey. The order to retreat was given, and the men began the long retracing of their trail to San Diego.

Retrace was, literally, what they did. Having noted the forest-filled canyons near Woodside, and reasoning that the way they came afforded the easiest pass over the coastal mountains, they returned to Sweeney Ridge, and then down the coast. The camps were approximately at the same sites as before, except that the first day's trip was short and took them only to a spot near Woodside, and on the Coastside, this time, camps were made at Tunitas Creek, Pescadero Creek, and Año Nuevo Creek.

A second careful search of the Monterey area was made, still without recognizing the bay, before the party resumed its southward march. After six more weeks of travel, the explorers joined their friends at San Diego, "smelling," as the Captain said, "of mule meat."

Portolá's failure to find Monterey, which loomed so large at the time, was eventually more than offset by his discovery of San Francisco Bay, but the true importance of this, the opening to the world of one of its finest harbors, was dismally slow in being recognized.

The discoverers, their senses dulled by weariness and hunger, had traversed, as chance would have it, both sides of the Peninsula, but only half-seeing its beauty and little realizing that, in time, it would be sought out by many thousands of people, over succeeding generations, as one of the world's finest places in which to live.

For the failure of this first expedition to recognize Monterey nobody can justly be held blameworthy when all the facts are considered, particularly the fact that the description they had of the haven was written by a sailor, whereas they viewed it only as overland travelers.

The glowing description they had brought with them was found in a book compiled by the pilot, Cabrera Bueno, and drawn from information found in the journals of the Vizcaíno expedition of 1602-3. It said, among other things, ". . . there is a good anchorage, clear and sheltered from all winds except from the northwest."

Strictly speaking, from a sailor's point of view, this statement was not inaccurate, yet it created almost inevitably in the mind of one who had never seen the place a vision of a nearly-enclosed harbor. But everyone who has entered Monterey by land knows that no such body of water appears. On the contrary, no matter what the angle of approach, one seems to be facing only a stretch of open sea.

Portolá's first approach to the area had been via the Salinas River Valley, as he came northward from San Diego. Knowing they were in the latitude where Monterey should be, the party had then spent three days searching the Point of Pines, Carmel Valley, and farther south, for a harbor that would seem to fit their image of Monterey. Concluding there must have been some mistake, they made the dutiful decision, after a thorough discussion in council, to extend their search farther north.

With supplies running low, with the winter rains soon to come, and with 17 of their men disabled by scurvy and dysentery, the choice was not lightly made.

Keeping close to the coast, it was October 23, 1769, when they entered what is now San Mateo County, by descending to the beach to by-pass the crumbling Sierra Blanca, or Chalk Mountain, as it has since been called, then climbing to a "mesa of level land that turns northwest by north." Proceeding in this direction they camped for the night at Gazos Creek.

The next day's march was unusually long—past Bean Hollow with its lagoon, Pescadero and Pomponio Creeks, and on to San Gregorio Creek. This trek exhausted them, and since Captain Rivera also had become a victim of the common illness, they took three days off for a rest.

The next night's camp was on *Purísima* Creek (which American usage has made Purissima) where some abandoned Indian huts looked interesting to the men, until they found themselves infested with fleas. They dubbed the place *Villa de las Pulgas* (Flea-town), which may have given rise to the later naming of a land grant, *Rancho de las Pulgas,* though the rancho was over the mountains, on the opposite side of the Peninsula. Another day took them to Pilarcitos Creek, on which now stands the town of Half Moon Bay, or possibly to near-by Frenchman Creek, where another rest was taken because the Commander himself was ill. Here the sighting of Pillar Point made them begin to wonder if they had passed Monterey.

Resuming the march after two days' rest, by nightfall they were at the foot of Montara or San Pedro Mountain. This high barrier with its steep cliffs and Devil's Slide could not be by-passed, so the next day's task was the climb to the summit. Their arrival at the top, fortunately on a clear day, afforded them a striking view, but that was not all—it brought them to the most crucial and dramatic moment in their entire journey.

Below them, running directly north, lay a straight stretch of white beach; then the coast line turned abruptly northwest and ended on the far horizon in a high promontory which they tentatively, and correctly, identified as Point Reyes.

But was it? Could it possibly be Monterey? If it was indeed Point Reyes, then the stretch of ocean that lay between it and the point on which they stood was the Bay of San Francisco, which had been so named on sailing charts ever since the days of Rodríguez Cermenho (1595). Also, if this was true, then certainly Monterey was somewhere behind them.

The seascape, including the *Farallón* Islands to the westward, was clearly visible from where they stood, but the true Bay of San Francisco was still concealed by higher hills to the east of them; and, likewise hidden from their view, was the Golden Gate to the northward.

After much gazing and puzzled discussion, they moved on down the hill, still wrestling with their problem, to camp in Pedro Valley where we found them at the beginning of our story. From there, Ortega was sent ahead to find out the truth of their whereabouts; and to this camp the hunters brought the first news of the "immense arm of the sea" just over the hill.

Thus, through a comedy of errors which was anything but comic to the explorers themselves, the great Bay of San Francisco was made known to the world—stumbled upon by an overland party instead of by sailors seeking its magnificent shelter.

Why seamen had never found it in two hundred years of sailing by is not difficult to explain—and the celebrated San Francisco fog is only one of the reasons. Everyone who has ever sailed out through the Golden Gate agrees that once outside, the Gate seems to close behind them. Even in the fairest of weather, the islands in the Bay and the Berkeley hills beyond seem so to blend with the coastal hills, rising sharply from the water's edge, as to create the appearance of a continuous coastline. Furthermore, the Farallón Islands through the centuries have stood off shore like a sentinel, causing every sailor worth his salt to keep to the west of them for safety's sake.

Portolá did not give up after his first attempt to find Monterey. Almost immediately he undertook a second expedition from San Diego, this time by both sea and land, which resulted in the positive identification of Monterey Bay, even to the oak tree near the beach that Vizcaíno had mentioned in 1602. So now (1770) a settlement was founded, from which further exploration of the Bay Area would be made.

With this much accomplished, Captain Portolá, who was a professional soldier of noble rank and only recently out from Spain, considered his California mission ended. He resigned the governorship and returned to Mexico. But authorities in Mexico City, particularly the great new Viceroy, Antonio Bucareli, ordered further investigation of the northern "estuary."

This whole movement to found settlements in Upper California, a region which Spain had claimed as hers for two hundred years, was a defensive maneuver, prompted by activities of England and Russia in the Pacific Ocean. These aggressive powers would not long respect Spain's claim to this attractive coast if it was not visibly occupied.

The process of occupying it was Spain's usual one. Centuries of experience had taught the Spaniards that nothing was more effective in assimilating new territory than a chain of missions for the conversion and civilizing of the natives. So, in California, Portolá's task had been to superintend the founding of missions—with fortified posts (*presidios*) to protect them—and his partner in the enterprise was the now famous missionary statesman, Fra Junípero Serra.

Previous planning for the mission chain had included a northern fortified outpost at Point Reyes, but the discovery of a possible new harbor to the north of Monterey forced a reconsideration. If this were, in fact, a good harbor, perhaps it, instead of Point Reyes, should be the northern outpost; if not, at least a way around it must be found.

Pedro Fages, now a captain and in full command, was sent to investigate. Starting from Monterey, he made two attempts to get around the Bay, and although Carquinez Strait stopped him, this inland channel, in itself, was an important discovery. And he is to be credited with at least two others. First, he blazed an easier, inland route from Monterey to the Bay via the later town of Gilroy, and second, the view he reported from the Berkeley hills made him the first explorer to give anything like an accurate description of the Bay and its now-famous entrance, the Golden Gate.

This report could not fail to strengthen in the Viceroy's mind the idea that the entrance to this new-found harbor might well be the place to fortify. To further investigate this possibility, Portolá's other principal officer, Captain Fernando Rivera, was chosen. First to purposely explore the Peninsula, he made his entry in 1774, bringing as his chaplain and diarist the man who was to become California's earliest historian and the founder of Mission Dolores, Father Francisco Palou.

As this party approached the Bay over Fages' inland route, Palou tells us that Rivera hailed as a familiar landmark the *palo alto* where he had camped with Portolá while Ortega explored the East Bay region. This tree is still a familiar landmark in A. D. 1963, but it is becoming less spectacular, being hidden by faster-growing trees around it. But to drivers headed southward on El Camino Real it is still noticeable; all the way from Atherton through Menlo Park it seems to stand in the middle of the road, directly ahead.

It is in Palou's journal of this expedition (1774) that the term *palo alto* first appears. Rivera, orienting his route by this landmark, as many travelers were to do after him, unwittingly determined the route of an important segment of the American West's oldest road—El Camino Real.

Palou, for his part, was deeply impressed with this spot for another reason: he considered it an excellent site for a mission, so much so that he marked it by erecting a large wooden cross.

As the party proceeded northward up the Peninsula, Rivera became concerned lest the sloughs on his right should block his advance, so he turned westward, shifting his route to the valley now filled with lakes, which he had traveled before. His hope was to find a hill top on the upper part of the Peninsula from which he could determine the lay of the land, but due to the lateness of the season (November, 1774), he was hampered by fog and rain. After leaving the valley, which he and Palou named *San Andrés* (Americans have made it San Andreas), the party spent several very uncomfortable days waiting for the weather to clear.

But, finally, came a sunny day, and Rivera and Palou made their way northward past San Francisco's Ocean Beach and climbed to the site of Fort Miley, overlooking the present Cliff House and Seal Rocks. From the view at this point Palou wrote the first detailed and accurate description of the Peninsula, the Golden Gate, the Farallones, and all the rest of the grand scene. This report, when it reached the heads of state in Mexico, convinced them that the tip of this Peninsula was undoubtedly the place for a presidio and a mission.

But one more step in exploration was needed to remove all uncertainty. Here was apparently a great harbor, but no ship had yet tested its entrance or its anchorage. To chart the Bay and its possibilities, a joint expedition by sea and land was ordered, and in August, 1775, Lieut. Juan Manuel Ayala, in command of the ship *San Carlos,* made the first entrance through the Golden Gate, and anchored for his surveying work off Angel Island.

About six weeks were spent in mapping the Bay, with the aid of a dugout canoe that had been cut from a redwood tree in Monterey. The south portion of the Bay was surveyed by Juan Bautista Aguirre, and the north portion, or San Pablo Bay, by José Cañizares.

The overland part of the expedition, under command of a sea captain, Bruno Heceta, and accompanied by Father Palou, was delayed for lack of personnel and

PENINSULA INDIANS, called by the Spaniards *Costaños* (Coast People), made boats of tightly-bundled tules. Feathered headdresses completed their ceremonial attire. LUDOVIK CHORIS, official artist with a Russian expedition, visited the Bay Area in 1816. His sketches of local life were published in Paris.

failed to arrive in time to make contact with Ayala. No diary of this expedition has been found, though Palou undoubtedly wrote one. We know, however, that the party camped by Lake Merced, and named it after the day in the religious calendar (September 24) on which they left it; and we are reasonably certain that Bruno Heceta named the San Bruno Mountains after his own patron saint.

The following year (1776) saw the actual founding of the long-proposed mission and presidio of San Francisco. The man assigned to carry out this important project was one of Spain's most capable army officers, and one with long experience on the north Mexican frontier, Col. Juan Bautista de Anza. Volunteer soldier-settlers with their families were recruited by him personally from the Sinaloa region, outfitted by the government, and brought to California to form the San Francisco Presidio garrison.

But before gathering the people, Anza's first assignment was to explore a practicable route of communication from Sonora on the Mexican mainland across the Colorado River and the Imperial Desert to the new California missions. Lower California, from whence had come the first settlers, was too poor to furnish all of the needed supplies and personnel, and travel northward by sea was fraught with many difficulties caused by adverse winds and currents.

Anza began by establishing friendly relations with the Yuma Indians on the Colorado River, then he probed the unknown western desert. His first sally was a failure—sand dunes and lack of water forced him back; but on the second attempt, by swinging farther south he succeeded in reaching the mountains, where water and pasture were plentiful. Finally he found his way to the San Gabriel Mission. He had opened a gateway to the new California, which he improved on the return trip by finding a shorter route. Though the gateway was later closed by a horrible massacre, it was held open long enough for the founders of San Francisco to come through.

Anza's crowning feat was the conducting of his party of 240 men, women, and children with hunderds of horses and mules and some 300 head of cattle, from Sonora, Mexico, to Monterey, California. He did it with the loss en route of but one human life (which was unavoidable) and a net increase in numbers by several births along the way.

When the party arrived at Monterey, Fernando Rivera, who was now Governor, apparently motivated by personal jealousy of Anza, refused to permit the making of the settlement, so Anza, leaving his people at Monterey, went on with a small party of soldiers and Father Pedro Font, his chaplain and diarist, to look over the site by the great Bay where his pioneer families were to settle.

This fast-riding detachment traveled directly to the head of the Peninsula via the route of today's El Camino Real, and selected the spots where the presidio and the mission should be built. Prevented by Rivera from doing more, Anza returned to Mexico, leaving his settlers under the care of Lieut. José Moraga.

When Anza was gone, and when orders from the Viceroy prevented further delay, authorization for the settlement was given, and Moraga set out with his charges for their ultimate destination. Moving with caution, the party arrived at San Mateo Creek, and the main body waited there three days while scouts examined the mission site to make sure there was still an ample supply of water. Finally, on June 27, 1776, at 6:30 A. M., they all set out for the last short leg of their journey, and by 7:30 P. M. they were making camp on the chosen site for the mission.

To the Indians on the Peninsula, this expedition was something new. By now they had become accustomed to seeing parties of white men traveling hither and yon, but never before had they seen white women and children, or cattle. The simple savages must have deduced from the presence of whole families that these people had come to stay, and although they could not guess why, they doubtless saw in all this something ominous for them.

But the Spaniards in coming meant them no harm; they had come to found a mission, and a mission was a benevolent institution. With Spaniards, missions on their frontiers had long since been taken as a matter of course, and the soldiers sent along to protect them were not thought of as being hostile to the natives.

The world of the Eighteenth Century had not yet learned to frown on conquest or colonialism, or on the use of missions as a means of conquest. The Spaniards even prided themselves in that thus they were serving both God and the King. As for the *padres* who operated the missions under government protection, if someone had suggested to them that their religious endeavors were being used as a means to a political end, they probably would have insisted that rather the contrary was true—that they, under God, were using both King and Empire as a means to the higher end of saving souls.

In preparation for their work in California, the Franciscan friars who traveled with the exploring parties considered themselves also explorers in their own right, studying the natives who were soon to be their proteges. What manner of people were they? Discovery of this sort was for them no less important, certainly, than the finding of new harbors or the opening of new transit routes.

Father Crespi, as he came with Portolá, noted in his journal each contact with the natives; he was impressed with their friendliness and the kinds of food they brought as gifts to the strangers: cakes of seeds and acorns, honey, fruit like a plum, and acorn porridge.

And he was on the lookout for suitable mission sites. Before anyone in the party had heard of San Francisco Bay, he had spotted two places he thought were good: the lagoon at Bean Hollow, south of Pescadero, and the wide San Gregorio Valley. He purposely gave to these places names, San Pedro Regalado and Santo Domingo, which he thought would be appropriate in case either of them should become the name of a mission.

But the padre who most carefully filled his journal with detailed information about the aborigines was Palou. His account, all unconsciously, betrays both his eager interest in every new sight along the way and his instinctive love for the childlike natives.

The late Professor A. L. Kroeber, a modern anthropologist, probably summarized correctly the opinion of most observers when he said the Indians here were "dark, dirty, squalid, and apathetic", but as Palou saw them they were "well-formed, tall, many of them a reddish color, and as bearded as any Spaniard".

He noted that the men went completely naked except for an occasional cape of animal skins, and when traveling in cold weather they sometimes carried fire-brands for warmth. The women wore aprons before and behind, and capes over their shoulders.

He repeatedly wrote that the men were "gentle, friendly, well-featured", and he talked to them in the Monterey language which they seemed to understand except when he tried to tell them about God and salvation. But they did not resist his making on them the sign of the cross. The natives seemed to reciprocate the warmth of his friendship by flocking around him, and one young man followed him for most of two days, calling himself his son, weeping much of the time, and parting finally with great sorrow.

As they traveled up the Peninsula, Palou was intrigued because "at every step we came to paths well-beaten by heathen" leading from the hills to the Bay, and, boy-like, he longed to follow one of them "to see what there is on the shore". But Captain Rivera refused to permit delays for such trivia. His assignment was to explore the Peninsula as a possible place for settlement, and as the season was already late, he feared being hampered by rain.

The Indian trails that so excited Palou's curiosity were important in a way that he probably did not realize—as a means of understanding the life of these natives. They told how the Bayside Indians obtained one of the staples of their diet, shellfish. They also explained the shell mounds that through the ages have marked the sites of their villages. Many hundreds of these refuse heaps once dotted the Peninsula and the rest of the Bay area, some of them having become hills twenty or more feet in height, containing within them the remains of human life over a period of some three or four thousand years.

In them were found the burials, the fire pits and the artifacts that offer the best clues to the kind of life these first inhabitants led. Undisturbed mounds are now rare but many back yards and gardens still contain in the soil the broken bits of of shells that mark the sites of ancient habitation.

Nature on the California coast, particularly in the Bay region, was perhaps overly kind to its inhabitants; its mild climate required only a minimum of shelter and created no season of scarcity for which people must prepare in order to survive. Besides the seasonal seeds and acorns, and the delicacies that could be had by hunting and fishing, the shellfish were available the year around with a minimum of effort.

In this paradise, it was not necessary to farm, hence the natives had no domesti-cated plants. They did, however, develop high skill in basketry which, with them, took the place of pottery and was also the nearest thing they did to weaving. Certain types of their baskets were made to hold water and in them they cooked their acorn meal by the device of dropping heated rocks into the basket. This, of course, was after first grinding the acorns in stone bowls and using a more porous basket or a bowl of sand to leach the bitter acid out of the meal.

Houses were made by first digging a hole in the ground the size of the dwelling, then erecting over it a dome-shaped frame and thatching it with *tules* or grass. Often the sweat house, at least in the larger villages, was the central feature—a hut large

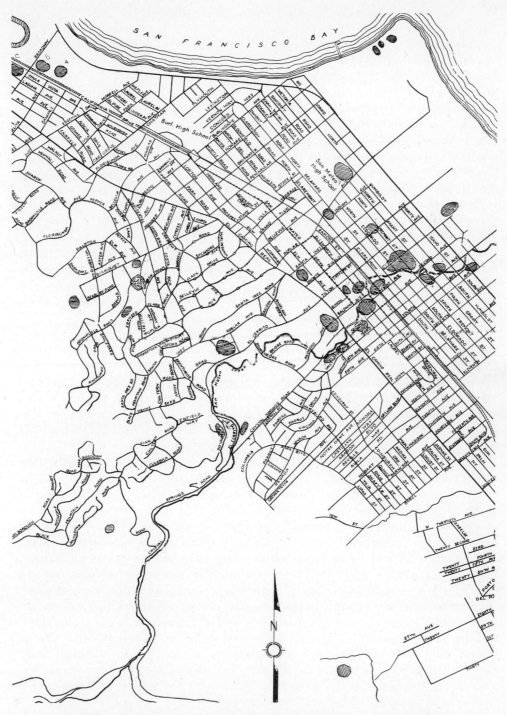

Indian shell mounds in Burlingame and San Mateo, as mapped by
Jerome Hamilton. Hundreds of such mounds once dotted the
Peninsula.

LAST COSTAÑO? Pedro Evencio (above). His father, as a neophyte, was made headman at San Mateo. Pedro's son, José (right), was "Indian Joe" of Coyote Point. See page 31.

enough to hold all the men, sometimes for ceremonial purposes, or on other occasions to cure ailments by the Turkish bath method. A fire inside, with water dropped on heated rocks, furnished the steam; then, after a good sweat, came a dousing in the cold creek outside.

Boats were made of tules or reeds from the marshlands tied in many bundles to form a raft which floated, not by keeping the water out, but because of the lightness of the material. They were propelled about the Bay, sometimes even out to sea, by means of a two-bladed paddle.

Tools and implements were of stone, bone, horn or shell: stone axes or hammers with dents for finger grip, bone scrapers, awls and cutting tools; there were horns and shells for digging, and shell for various other things, especially jewelry which doubtless served also as trading goods. Stone bowls for grinding acorns are still commonly found which had to be shaped by endless grinding with sand and hard rock. The most intricate work with rock, however, was in the making of the smoothly shaped and polished charm stones for the medicine man's magic, and in chipping arrowheads. Common weapons were the bow and arrow and sometimes stone-headed darts, which Palou said were very well made.

The inhabitants of this area were known by the Spaniards as the *Costaños* or Coast People—a regional group that spoke a more or less common language, living in the territory extending from the Golden Gate and Carquinez Strait southward beyond Monterey and Soledad, and eastward to the Coast Range marked by Mount Diablo and Mount Hamilton. In this territory there were, according to Kroeber's estimate, perhaps 7,000 people. Other anthropologists claim evidence of larger numbers.

Social and family ties in this easy-going society were loosely held. Marriages were easily made and as easily broken, and a man might marry all the sisters of a family—perhaps even include his mother-in-law. Villages had their chiefs but the position was secured rather by talent for leadership than by formal election, though hereditary rights to it were recognized.

Besides a common language, the Costaños had a common mythology built mainly around the coyote, the eagle, and the humming bird, but it also encompassed other less tangible spirits that were invoked by ceremonial dances with whistles and percussion noise makers. Palou noted that when he gave these Indians tobacco they smoked it with ceremonial gestures of blowing the smoke upward and by passing the pipe from mouth to mouth in order of individual rank.

The simple people in this area were among the first in California to feel the impact of the white man's coming. Seven missions were established in their territory at which native cultural elements were soon forgotten; and the mission era was followed by a wholesale granting of land to private owners who used the natives as laborers. Hence, for good or ill, the Costaños were among the first in the world of California aborigines to lose their cultural identity.

Mission Outpost at San Mateo (William H. Dougal)

# II. Mission Days: *Church, State, and Neophytes*

*"Spain sent here her best."*   NELLIE VAN DE GRIFT SANCHEZ

If the founders of San Francisco had known the facts about the Golden Gate's climate they probably would have placed the first mission at San Mateo, or perhaps at Palou's favorite site in the Menlo Park-Palo Alto area; certainly not where it is in San Francisco.

The requirements for a good mission site were well known. There must be accessibility to large numbers of heathen; availability of wood and water; plenty of good grazing land; and, particularly, good soil and climate for the growing of food crops. A successful mission would have many hundreds of neophytes in training and must be able to feed them.

On this last point the San Francisco mission site failed completely to pass the test. When the Mission was twenty-five years old, a visiting German scientist noted that in its garden there were only "a few stunted trees, which scarcely bore any fruit," and "the only things that grow well in the garden are asparagus, cabbage, and several sorts of salad, onions and potatoes". The missionaries had, in fact, learned long before this that their farming had to be done twelve to fifteen miles down the Peninsula where there was less fog and the weather was generally warmer.

This mistake in selecting the site, if mistake it can be called, was a natural one. The Presidio site, chosen by Col. Juan Bautista de Anza, was, of necessity, located to guard the harbor entrance, and his chaplain, Father Pedro Font, marked for the Mission the best site to be found near the Presidio. He had no way of knowing about the frequent chilling fog.

While this choice of a site saddled the Mission with a permanent handicap, in another respect it made interesting history. Because of it, the Presidio, an instrument of government, and the Mission, an arm of the Church, were tucked in together on a narrow peninsula, only three miles apart as the sea gull flies, where they and the natives were alone together on this far-north frontier. For the duration of the Spanish regime, this was their little world. Naturally, they got in each other's way from time to time, but they had to get along because together they must manage the natives.

17

In the record of this getting on together, they have given us an interesting sample—a laboratory specimen so to speak, isolated for study—not only of the life in California under Spain, but also of the working in the larger world of the famous Spanish partnership between Church and State.

Anyone who may wish to reconstruct the primitive scene of these events will not find it difficult. He has only to visit the small *adobe* remnant of the old Presidio overlooking the Golden Gate, now (1963) used as the United States Army officers' club, then take a somewhat circuitous drive through San Francisco streets to the well-preserved mission chapel on Dolores Street at Sixteenth. Meanwhile, in his imagination, he must shut out the Twentieth Century surroundings and substitute for them a winding trail through brushy hills, ravines and sand dunes, and, at the Mission, a group of buildings on the edge of a broad valley that then looked out on the Bay.

All this was, as we say it now, "*in* San Francisco", but when speaking of Spanish and Mexican times this phrase is meaningless. Not only was the entire Peninsula a single geographical unit (as it still is), but in those days it was treated as a unit, and the history of those times has to be seen in the same context. The territory of the San Francisco (Dolores) Mission extended to San Francisquito Creek, which is the present south boundary of San Mateo County; beyond this was the domain of Santa Clara Mission.

The settlement-founding party for San Francisco arrived at the Mission site on June 27, 1776, just a few days before an epoch-making event on the far-away opposite rim of the same continent—a matter having to do with a liberty bell, a declaration of independence, and the "Spirit of '76".

At San Francisco, Mission and Presidio were to be founded simultaneously—and for the purpose, under the command of Lieut. José Moraga, came a small garrison of soldiers and their families, two Franciscan friars (Palou and Father Pedro Cambón), plus servants, muleteers, and *vaqueros* (cowboys).

With them to this far-off frontier, besides their pack animals, they drove their staff of life—a herd of some three hundred head of cattle, belonging in part to the Mission and part to the Presidio, plus a few owned by individuals. The beef was to keep them alive and the hides to serve for almost everything else—beds, shelter, saddles, ropes, and the rawhide thongs that held everything together.

While the first temporary shelters were being erected, the two padres began the business of establishing friendly contacts with the natives. This work of theirs was to be no mere matter of preaching the gospel. As experienced missionaries, they well knew that, friendly though they might wish to be, all could not be permanently sweetness and light, although many versions of the mission story, as told today, make it appear to have been so. The thorough-going and wholesale transformation they expected to bring about in the lives of these savages would require a deftly mingled use of love and punishment; or to use a familiar figure, to make the donkey go they would need both the carrot and the whip.

They started by making the rounds of the near-by Indian villages with gifts of trinkets and food, and for some time their efforts seemed to be well rewarded. The Indians responded with many return visits to the mission encampment.

But on August 12 came the first setback. A war party from the Indian community on San Mateo Creek, down the Peninsula, attacked a village near the mission site, burned it, and so frightened the inhabitants that they took to their tule rafts and fled across the Golden Gate to the opposite shore, apparently not impressed by the Spaniards' offer to defend them. The San Mateo Indians were their traditional enemies and this raid was apparently designed to punish them for fraternizing with the newcomers. If so, it was effective, for it practically stopped all visiting at the Mission.

But friendship was, in time, restored; in fact, when it was renewed, the visitors began to get embarrassingly friendly. They grew familiar, took liberty with soldiers' wives, and became insolent. When repulsed for this, they retaliated by shooting arrows, and thereby brought the soldiers into action. The culprits were seized and whipped; for this, more arrows were shot, and then something like a battle with guns vs. arrows took place in which one Indian was killed and another wounded.

After this, there was no meeting at all for about three months but finally, in March, 1777, restrained but friendly contacts began again, and by June 24, three days short of a year after their arrival, the missionaries had the satisfaction of baptizing their first converts.

The young man of twenty and the two nine-year-old boys who took this important step probably understood very little of its religious significance, but they soon found that it brought about a marked change in their manner of living. They now took up residence at the Mission, where they had better food, with the new luxury of having it served to them regularly, wore clothes, and had better shelter than before. They also began training in the arts of their new way of life—learning to plant and care for crops, herd cattle and tan hides.

They found, in time, that their gentle masters, the missionaries, would put up with no nonsense and would hold them to the decision they had made. If they grew tired of the new work-a-day life, they were not permitted to change their minds and return to their old haunts. If they ran away, they were brought back and punished by the soldiers, which usually meant being whipped.

The padres found by experience that this form of punishment was in general most satisfactory—the stocks seemed more cruel, and to build an effective jail with the materials they had at hand in the beginning was impracticable. To administer this discipline and to protect the padres, a small detachment of men from the Presidio garrison was regularly quartered at the Mission. In the quaint words of the truthful mission historian, Father Zephyrin Engelhardt, the natives who became Christians "yielded their savage liberty to the service of their Creator under the direction of the missionaries."

But with all this, the new way must have had, on balance, greater attraction than the old, for by October, when the President of the Missions, Father Junípero Serra paid a visit, there were seventeen "new Christians", and from then on the number increased steadily.

With this increase came the growing problem of providing food. Of beef there was plenty, for the herds increased amazingly, but it soon became evident that grain, fruit, and vegetables, with few exceptions, could not be grown near the Mission. A better spot was soon discovered down the coast, however, some fifteen miles away, which they named San Pedro.

This was the valley where Portolá had camped. It is still known as Pedro Valley, although in 1957 it became a part of the city of Pacifica. Here there was more sunshine, the soil was good, and there were Indians to be converted.

Some of the Mission's very early converts came from this valley; each year there were more, and in 1783 the chief of the village was baptized. The site of this village is believed to be that of the present historic Sánchez Adobe. The padres reached eagerly for this valley. By 1786 they had built a granary there, a chapel, and rooms where they could stay during planting and harvest seasons; very soon they reported that *all* of the Mission's plantings were transferred there.

Early in 1787, glowing reports were written about the place. Surely it was a God-send, they said, and it probably meant that Divine Providence was leading them in this direction in order to bring about the conversion of the Indians down the coast. Their work and their comments during the next three or four years show that in their minds San Pedro held all their hopes for the Mission's future.

They built some 2,760 yards of fence with live willow posts, which they hoped would grow into a hedge, dug drainage ditches, and, each year, added something to the buildings. A typical year saw the growing of some thirty-six acres of wheat and eight or nine acres of corn, the planting of a pear and a peach tree, some vines and rosemary, and the beginning of a vineyard.

There were setbacks—the grizzly bears damaged the crops, and to save what they could they harvested early, only to see the grain spoil from being cut too soon— yet somehow things moved ahead. The first buildings were of the primitive *palizada* type (poles stuck upright in the ground, plastered with mud and roofed with thatch), but the later ones were of the more permanent adobe bricks, one such being a new granary 16 by 110 feet in size. The general plan of buildings, according to Spanish custom, was toward the ultimate forming of a closed quadrangle.

But one side of the quadrangle was still open when disaster struck the project. In the Mission records, reports on San Pedro mysteriously cease and for a clue to what happened we have only the record of baptisms and burials. Deaths at San Pedro, which were normally a dozen or so a year, leaped in 1791 to forty-seven, while baptisms, after a brief spurt upward, dropped to almost none.

This clearly indicates the beginning of a sad story that sooner or later all of the missions had to tell: an epidemic of a disease new to the Indians for which their bodies had no immunity. In such instances the community was usually seized with fright at the number of deaths and many, if not all, of those able to travel took refuge in flight.

For a small village this could mean annihilation, and after 1794 we hear almost nothing about San Pedro. The buildings slowly crumbled into ruins and apparently all else that remained were the cemetery, cattle roaming the hills, and possibly a little absentee farming.

This disaster at San Pedro was probably the beginning of what Father Engel-

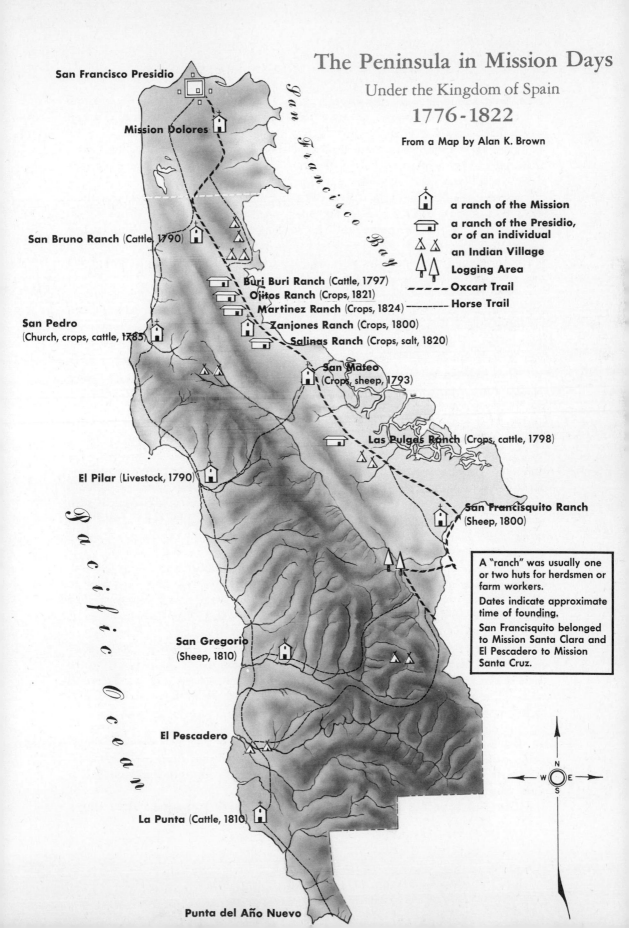

# The Peninsula in Mission Days

## Under the Kingdom of Spain

### 1776-1822

From a Map by Alan K. Brown

San Francisco Presidio

Mission Dolores

San Bruno Ranch (Cattle, 1790)

Buri Buri Ranch (Cattle, 1797)
Ojitos Ranch (Crops, 1821)
Martinez Ranch (Crops, 1824)
Zanjones Ranch (Crops, 1800)
Salinas Ranch (Crops, salt, 1820)

San Pedro
(Church, crops, cattle, 1785)

San Mateo
(Crops, sheep, 1793)

Las Pulgas Ranch (Crops, cattle, 1798)

El Pilar (Livestock, 1790)

San Francisquito Ranch
(Sheep, 1800)

San Gregorio
(Sheep, 1810)

El Pescadero

La Punta (Cattle, 1810)

Punta del Año Nuevo

San Francisco Bay

Pacific Ocean

**Legend:**
- a ranch of the Mission
- a ranch of the Presidio, or of an individual
- an Indian Village
- Logging Area
- ‑ ‑ ‑ ‑ Oxcart Trail
- ———— Horse Trail

A "ranch" was usually one or two huts for herdsmen or farm workers.

Dates indicate approximate time of founding.

San Francisquito belonged to Mission Santa Clara and El Pescadero to Mission Santa Cruz.

N
W E
S

Colonel Juan Bautista de Anza, in whose memory local historians
dedicated a monument in 1959 to commemorate the Anza Campsite
of 1776 on San Mateo Creek.

WILLIAM H. DOUGAL, Gold Rush artist-engraver, had a passion for accuracy. His upper view of Mission Dolores shows the broad road that is now Dolores Street; and in the distance, masts of ships stranded in Yerba Buena cove. The close-up view looks across Dolores Street.

23

hardt calls a "great mortality" at Mission Dolores which reached its height in 1795-96 and reduced the total neophyte population from 912 to 600. Several years elapsed before the loss was regained. No one seems to have identified the disease at this time but a later scourge was recognized as measles.

The loss at San Pedro turned the attention of the missionaries to San Mateo on the other side of the Peninsula. There the Indians were more numerous, and though hostile at first, seem to have been won over. About 1793 a substantial building of adobe bricks was erected there. This building became the victim of an earthquake, but it was superseded, probably about 1810, by a larger and more substantial one. This second building was some 35 by 112 feet in size, a story and a half high, and roofed with burnt tile. It stood until 1869 at the present corner of Baywood Avenue and El Camino Real.

San Mateo became a center for farming, salt gathering, and the handling of a large flock of sheep—the upper half-story of the building there being evidently designed for the storage of wool. Below were six compartments, one of which served as a chapel and the others for storage or habitation, and as an over-night stopping place for travelers. San Mateo, without doubt, replaced San Pedro as the center for all of the Mission's farming operations, and its importance to the Mission increased as the years passed.

Despite two other setbacks with disease, the whole number of neophytes climbed to well over a thousand and, in time, two other outposts were developed across the the waters of the Bay—one called San Pablo in the East Bay and the other San Rafael, on the Marin Peninsula, which later became an independent mission.

The livestock also increased, by many thousands. During the peak years of prosperity the reports show as many as 10,000 sheep at San Mateo, 10,740 head of cattle pastured in various places, and hundreds of horses and mules besides some goats and pigs. These animals grazed as far south as Purissima Creek, or perhaps even to Tunitas Creek on the Coastside, and down to San Francisquito Creek (Palo Alto) on the Bayside.

Crops were harvested in varying amounts according to the season, the record year being 1812 with an in-gathering of 11,098 bushels of grain, lentils, peas, beans, etc. Reports agree that this farming was done "in spots down the Peninsula".

All work was done by Indians who had been trained to handle oxen and a wooden plow, to plant with their own hands, to harvest with a sickle, and to thresh the grain by driving horses over it and winnowing it in the wind. Some had become herdsmen, some butchers; they had learned to cure hides, to cook down the fat into tallow and then mold it into candles. Other neophytes had learned to make adobe bricks and build walls, to burn tiles for the roof, and still others to cook, spin, weave, and do all the other work necessary to living in those times.

Two lone padres directed this entire enterprise, and it was they who had introduced all of these various skills, one by one, either by their own personal instruction or through craftsmen brought in for the purpose. The Indians thus became the labor force, both skilled and unskilled, for a self-supporting community—producing to supply all of their own essential needs. Not only was this the case at the Mission itself, but if a job was to be done at the Presidio, Indians did the work—either heathen hired or rounded up for the purpose, or a crew of neophyte (Christian) laborers sent over from the Mission.

Perhaps some of this was "forced labor" by standards of the Twentieth Century. But no one here at that earlier time had ever seen any other pattern of society than that of Europe, with its serfs and servant class, or Mexico with its peons. The Mission became a social and economic unit cast in the same mold, with its headmen, artisans, servants, and laborers. Its one great weakness was that it never reached the stage of being able to function without the padres.

The history of Mission Dolores, though it was by no means among the largest of the missions, serves well to illustrate another point, particularly for people of today who visit the missions and go away thinking of them only as churches. Church-centered they were, to be sure, but they became, even by modern standards of size, large ranches, and since there was very little they could purchase from the outside world, they had to be economically self-sufficient.

The growth of Mission Dolores did not fail to bring on some friction, locally, between Church and State. Very early, the padres became apprehensive about room on the Peninsula for their livestock, for by 1790 their cattle had increased from less-than-200 head with which they started to nearly 1,800, and with horses, mules and sheep, to a total of 3,600. In the same fourteen years the Presidio's herd had also grown, from 115 to 1,215.

Supposedly, each presidio in California had its own herd of cattle, known as the *Rancho del Rey* or King's Ranch; the King's cattle were branded with an "R" for *Rey* while the mission cattle wore an "F"·for *Franciscano*. At that time, very few cattle, if any, were owned by individuals—for the simple reason that everybody in the settlement was attached either to the Mission or to the Presidio.

Life at the Presidio as well as at the Mission depended directly on the cattle, and the presence of a large herd gave a sense of security. But as the herds grew, space did become a problem since by land-use standards of that time, in the semi-arid Peninsula climate, each animal required for its feed several acres of brush-free grass.

The missionaries pleaded that there was not room on this narrow Peninsula for two such large herds of cattle, and that it was not necessary to keep two, for the Presidio could just as well buy its beef and hides from the Mission. (Little or no use was made of the milk). Their arguments, pressed both locally and through their superiors in Mexico, were finally successful and in 1791 orders came to abandon the Rancho del Rey at San Francisco. The cattle were driven to Monterey and added to the King's herd there.

But this left the army men unhappy. It was not proper, they held, for the Supreme Government to be placed in a position of dependence on the Mission, and it was alleged that the padres at Dolores, taking advantage of their monopoly, charged the Presidio more than the generally-accepted price per head for beef even though their cattle were a third smaller than those at Monterey.

After five years without a government herd, Governor Diego Borica was persuaded to re-establish the Rancho del Rey at San Francisco. He ordered 265 head of cattle purchased from the Mission, and since everything had now spread southward down the Peninsula, he announced that the region known as Buri Buri, which would now include the cities of South San Francisco, San Bruno, Millbrae, and the northerly half of Burlingame, would be taken by the Presidio for its grazing land.

Against this, the padres protested with more pressure than ever, both on the familiar grounds that there was not room for the two herds (an argument which now lost some of its force since the Government, by purchasing its new herd from the Mission, would not increase the total number of cattle), and also because, said they, since the Mission existed for the Indians, to whom the land legally belonged, this taking of land that the Mission was using prejudiced the natural and legal rights of the natives.

Both sides carried their respective arguments to the highest authorities—the Franciscans to the heads of their order in Mexico, and the Governor to the Viceroy, whose word in the matter would be the final decision.

Before making his decision, the Viceroy called for a report from José Darío Argüello, a man on the ground who was familiar with the local geography. Argüello was then Commandant of the Presidio of San Francisco, and during his career he held positions of large responsibility for many years in one or the other of the Californias. His son, Luís, became Governor of Alta California under Mexico, and his family became owners of *Rancho de las Pulgas* in San Mateo County.

Argüello's report, which, of course, favored the Presidio's point of view, has an incidental interest for us because of the local place names it used. The taking of Buri Buri for the Government, as far west as the *Cañada de San Andrés* (now San Andreas Valley), would do the Mission no harm, he said, for there were six other good pasturing areas it could use.

One was San Pedro, and beyond it was *El Pilar* (near Half Moon Bay and Pillar Point). There were also *San Mateo* (south of Buri Buri), *San Bruno* (the San Bruno Mountains north of South San Francisco), and there were *La Visitación* (Visitacion Valley, since made famous by the nationally known Cow Palace), and *La Merced* (meaning the area around the lake of the same name). All of these still-familiar place names were in use as early as 1797.

The Government took Buri Buri, but the argument over land for the Presidio cattle did not cease. It went through several phases, and ended only when, under the Republic of Mexico, all enterprises by State or Church were sunk in a rising tide of private initiative. Then land grants to individuals became the order of the day.

Trouble of a more serious nature appeared in the mid-1790's when it became known that large numbers of neophytes at the Mission were running away, and the rumor was that Father Antonio Danti was causing it all by his overly-strict discipline, tight rationing of food, and severe punishments.

Mass disciplinary troubles at the missions were rare, considering the large numbers of Indians involved, but these same large numbers made any sign of discontent or insubordination dangerous. Runaway neophytes were a constantly recurring problem, but ordinarily not a serious one. Many came back of their own accord;

CULTURAL TRANSITION, recorded by Choris, shows a native ceremonial dance at Mission Dolores; and below, Indians playing a traditional game in the shadow of a mission building.

others were rounded up individually by the soldiers. But when large numbers deserted, Government officials as well as the missionaries were concerned.

A crisis occurred when Father Danti, probably sensitive about criticism of his regime, instead of asking the soldiers to go after the large number that had fled to the East Bay, sent a group of fourteen trusted neophytes to persuade the prodigals to return.

To everyone's surprise, the expedition met with such angry resistance, both by the pagans and the Christian Indians living in that area, that half of the men sent were killed. This news reached the ears of Governor Borica but he decided to do nothing about it at the moment, for fear of stirring up more trouble among the hostile natives on that side of the Bay, who were already a potential threat to Mission San José to the south of them.

But when, a few months later, two hundred neophytes took off, including some of the most stable and trusted ones, the Governor ordered an investigation. He probably did not know at the time that the flight of the larger group was mainly due to the already-mentioned sickness and "great mortality" at the Mission.

Many neophytes were called to testify in the investigation. The Governor wanted to know: was it true that the desertions were caused by Father Danti's severity and his "cruel" punishments? Many witnesses testified to what, if true, were shocking instances of cruelty and to insufficient food served at the Mission. On the other hand, historian Engelhardt explains that many of the runaways took off for reasons no more serious than "the inclination of male converts to run away in order to gratify their animal propensities. Nor would they scruple", he continues, "to put the blame for their waywardness on their missionary benefactors".

The president of the Missions at the time, Father Fermín Lasuén, also defended Danti, pointing out that the large number of converts disproved the charge of cruelty. Nevertheless, the Governor was evidently convinced that at least some of the blame rested with Father Danti for he ordered the soldiers at the Mission not to aid in punishing any neophytes unless asked to do so by *both* of the friars. He also wrote to Father President Lasuén, insisting on better treatment and better food at San Francisco, and to this Lasuén assented.

Affairs of this kind could be dangerous because of the encouragement they gave to hostile tribes that were always in the offing. In this instance, it finally became necessary to send a punitive military expedition into the East Bay to forestall attacks on Mission San José.

But as the missionizing process spread over an ever-widening area, this danger diminished. Native villages were abandoned, one by one, as their people were baptized and moved to the mission centers. Recalcitrant individuals who would not go along with the majority went to live with other unconverted tribes, or fled to the hills and became roving bandits.

Occasionally, one of those rebellious individuals, who placed a high value on his savage freedom, became a thorny problem, and probably the most famous of these was Pomponio. His story begins about 1801 when a large group of youngsters was brought to Mission Dolores for baptism, mainly from an Indian village near Bolinas Bay, now in Marin County. One of these was an infant named Lupugrium.

As was customary, the padres gave to each Indian when baptized a Christian (i.e. European) name, attached to his native name. Finding names became somewhat of a chore after the baptisms ran into the hundreds, and as the list of saints became overworked, the priests dipped into classical history. This particular child came up with a name that was a mixture of Spanish, Roman and American Indian: José Pomponio Lupugrium. But he was known, and became notorious, as Pomponio.

Only the barest facts of his life are known. He grew up as a neophyte, showed great promise, and demonstrated ability as a leader. In 1816 he was put in a position of responsibility at the San Rafael outpost. But he abused his power; some kind of a crisis occurred, and he ran away. Embittered by these experiences, he remained an incorrigible renegade.

He was, indeed, a leader. He formed a group of desperados, drawn from the dissidents of various missions, who called themselves the *Insurgentes,* and waged a campaign of robbery and murder. Most of Pomponio's victims were Indians but he killed at least one Spanish soldier, and committed other depredations, mainly southward in the area of Mission Soledad. But in the summer of 1823 he had his headquarters in the vicinity of Alpine Creek in the present San Mateo County.

In this way his name has become immortalized on the map by the Coastside stream that since his time has been called Pomponio Creek. Also, the ridge at the head of this creek was once called *Cuchillo de Pomponio* or Pomponio Ridge. There was once a country school that bore his name, and even a Boy Scout camp does him honor!

Stories about him say he was at various times made prisoner and escaped—one such, probably not true, relating that he cut off his own heels to free his feet from the shackles that held him. He was finally captured in Novato Canyon north of San Rafael and taken to Monterey for trial by court martial.

Unfortunately, the record of his trial, which could have given us more information about him, was destroyed in the San Francisco fire of 1906. He was convicted and executed by a firing squad in 1824. By the Indians in general he was ever afterward regarded as a hero—a kind of Joaquín Murieta of his day—and his story has become a part of California's folklore of bad men.

A folk tale of an entirely different sort is the story of *La Vieja*. It is authenticated by the fact that in the official record of Mexican land grants, Tiburcio Vásquez's grant is described as extending inland from the coast up Pilarcitos Creek as far as a "hill called *La Vieja*".

Bluntly translated, *La Vieja* simply means the Old Woman, a curious name for a hill. Some of the late elderly descendants of local Spanish families, who remembered the term as being in common use, readily identified the hill that was known by this name.

"The Old Woman", it seems, was an Indian who lived on the Coastside, probably at El Pilar, a mission ranch near the present Half Moon Bay. The story about her is simply this: she became very ill and the *vaqueros* at the ranch were puzzled, not knowing what to do. They felt they must do something—she meant that much to them—and the only thing they could think of was to get her to the Mission, or at least to the outpost at San Mateo, where help could be had.

They probably carried her, somehow, on horseback (these vaqueros could do almost anything on a horse), but after traveling up Pilarcitos Creek, the route of the present road from Half Moon Bay to San Mateo, they got only as far as the round hill they had to climb to get over the ridge, when they discovered that *La Vieja* had died on their hands. So they dug a grave and buried her there at the foot of the hill.

This is the story that was told and retold until the hill itself came to be called The Old Woman. People on the Coastside remarked, when there was an east wind, "It's blowing down off *La Vieja* today," and men went to look for the cattle "up by *La Vieja*." Vásquez had confidence enough in the permanence and familiarity of the name to use it as an identifying landmark for the corner of his property.

What was there about the incident, or about the woman herself, that could cause her name to become a legend and her monument a hill? Was it some superstitious fear growing out of the extraordinary circumstance of her death? Or was she an extraordinary person? At least the story seems to indicate that, by her time, Christian influence had penetrated far enough so that when faced with the tragedy of sickness and death the boys turned for help to the Mission instead of to the witch doctor.

The story of the Mission and its neophytes must end, unfortunately, with a melancholy note. One severe epidemic played havoc with the Indians because the disease, whatever it may have been, was new to them. The second such scourge, which came in 1804-1807, was recognized as measles. It wrought death and terror among the neophytes and reduced the mission population from 1,103 to 828.

But worse things were to come. From 1812 to 1817 there was another plague which brought the numbers down from 1,224 to 1,060, and this time it was no mere epidemic. The basic trouble was identified as syphilis. This disease had so weakened the Indians, and become so wide-spread among them, that the slightest maladies caused many deaths.

Father Engelhardt quotes a French writer of 1817 who said, "There was not a single mission where the births were equal to the deaths," then adds his own qualification: "This was true of sixteen out of the nineteen existing missions. Mission Dolores belonged to those that reported more deaths than births. It was the zealous Fr. Ramón Abella of San Francisco," he goes on, "who, on being instructed to offer a reason for this sad state of things to the governor, gave it as his conviction that the decrease was chiefly due to the *Mal Galico*." This term, meaning the French disease, was then the common name for syphilis.

It was with this tragic accompaniment that the drama of Spain's rule on this Peninsula came to an end. Although the number of neophytes temporarily picked up again, the Costaño Indians were still a dying race when the winning of national independence by Mexico, of which California was a part, rang down the curtain on the story of Spain in California. As in a Shakespearean tragedy, or a grand opera, the last scene closed with all of the main characters either dead or dying on the stage.

In this drama, the leading roles were played by the Spanish State, the Church, as represented by the missions, and the Natives. The fact of Mexican independence from

Spain (1821) annihilated the Spanish State in California, and as for the missions, the long Latin American struggle for independence (roughly 1810 to 1825) had cut off their financial support, and neither the people of Mexico in general nor of California in particular showed any enthusiasm for maintaining them. On the contrary, the tendency was to eye with envy the wealth that the missions were supposed to have accumulated, especially the lands they were using.

The padres, of course, tried to carry on, but these were not men of the calibre of the earliest priests, and their position was next to impossible, in any event. With neither financial nor popular support, morale at the missions sank and they soon lost their hold on the natives. Of those attached to Mission Dolores, the neophyte population dropped quickly from 1,100 to slightly over 200, where it stayed for a decade.

When Mission Dolores was secularized (1835) it ceased to be a mission and became, in theory, a parish church. This meant that all control that the missionaries had exercised over the Indians was abolished, except that of a purely spiritual or personal nature, and it further meant that the physical properties were taken over by the Government and placed under an administrator.

In theory, the neophytes were to be organized in a self-governing *pueblo,* under the direction of the administrator, with their own *alcaldes* and other officers. But, instead, they were simply told by the administrator that they were now "his Indians." Also, under the law, they were supposed to receive land on which to make themselves self-supporting, but nothing of the kind was ever done.

In 1839 William E. P. Hartnell, inspecting the missions for the Mexican Government, found only eighty Indians supposedly attached to Mission Dolores but living at San Mateo. Three years later there were seventy-eight who were by then "scattered all over the peninsula." Further light on their situation is cast by Theodore Hittell's comment that at least some of them "were employed by private persons, and many against their will. In other words, they were held as slaves, and not as voluntary servants."

The fortunes of this remnant of aborigines apparently did not improve much with the coming of Americans to California. Early American settlers in San Mateo found a squalid camp of Indians by San Mateo Creek, but it seems that when William D. M. Howard took over this property he ordered them off.

The United States census of 1860 listed sixty-two persons on the Peninsula classified as Indians born in California. Their occupations were given as laborers, woodchoppers, herdsmen, and servants. Twenty-one of them were minors, eight of whom were attached to Spanish families and thirteen to American families. Their status in the family was not specified. Twenty-seven Indians seem to have had households of their own, constituting nine families.

In the late 1930's an Ishi-like "character" known as Indian Joe was living in a crude shelter under the trees on Coyote Point, earning a little money by guarding people's boats. Some said he was disagreeable and suspicious; others said this was not true. His real name, it seems, was Joseph (José) Evencio.

If this identification was correct, Indian Joe's grandfather was baptized as a child at the Mission and became a neophyte named Evencio Gessmon, the latter probably being his native Indian name. In manhood he was made Headman of the neophytes at San Mateo and lived until after 1846. His son, Indian Joe's father, was Pedro Evencio, born in the 1820's and killed by a train in about the year 1900. He is shown in a photograph of the 1890's living in a neat shack in San Mateo and appears to have been a man of character and personality.

Indian Joe disappeared with the building of the Merchant Marine school on Coyote Point during World War II, and it is assumed he is now dead. It appears that, with his passing, the race that first inhabited the Peninsula, the people whose rising smokes attracted the attention of the first white explorers, became extinct. Ironically, but too often true, the nation that brought them Christianity and civilization brought also the diseases that killed them off.

It was not that their lot was harder than that of other Indians of the Western Hemisphere. In fact, the impact of European invasion was gentler here than in most other areas. But these simple people had neither the physical stamina nor the strength of large numbers with which to survive the ordeal; nor did they have the wit or resourcefulness to adjust to a new way of life and make a place for themselves in a world so different from their own.

Cattle roping in mission days.

Coastal grazing country.

# III. Rancheros: *Land hunger in two patterns*

*"A goodly people were these Californians. Generous to a fault, hospitable, rich in lands and herds."*     MAJOR HORACE BELL

November 5, 1835 was a great day in the life of José Antonio Sánchez, for it was the day on which he received title to his land grant, the famous *Rancho Buri Buri*. A life-long soldier and junior officer at the Presidio, and now a country squire and patriarchal head of a large family clan, this was a fitting climax to his career.

The valuable property that was now his stretched from the San Bruno Mountains to Rancho San Mateo and from the salt marsh of the Bay to the San Andreas Valley. Ownership of it would make his own social position secure and it would give to his family top economic rating in the new world that was then coming into being.

Unlike the tight regime of old Spain, free trade under the Mexican Republic was now bringing to the California coast ships from Boston and Liverpool, laden with attractive goods: gay shawls, dresses and draperies, up-to-date wearing apparel for men, furniture, cutlery, tools, glass, and many other luxuries hitherto all but unknown. Ability to buy these things was the badge of affluence, and to get them one needed the hides and tallow that only large herds of cattle could produce—and cattle require land.

Sánchez, like all the other men of his community and generation, was hungry for land. Indeed, it was largely land hunger—that powerful human appetite that has made so much history around the globe—that put an end to the mission era in order that the hungry ones might lay hands on the vast acreage the missions were using.

At the same time, in another part of the continent, land hunger of a different pattern was at work—there it was pushing the Anglo-American frontier westward. And the Manifest Destiny of this frontier was soon to bring it into conflict with Spanish-type land holdings in California.

But Sánchez and his neighbors, quite unaware of this far-off threat, pressed for their version of self-realization—their pattern of land ownership. They coveted also and, in fact, took over along with the land, the labor force to be had in the mission-trained Indians. In justification, they argued that the missions had now finished their work as missions and should henceforth confine themselves to performing the religious functions of parish churches.

In his younger days, Sánchez had had no reason to question the obvious fact that large herds of cattle were for the State and the Church alone, and his job had been to serve the one and protect the other. Now he saw emerging a world of private enterprise. Land was being granted to individuals—not many as yet and only in the outlying areas beyond the ranchos the Mission had used. But with the decline and, finally, the secularization of the Mission, and the even more rapid liquidation of the government herd of cattle (the former Rancho del Rey), he had been able to get Buri Buri, right in the center of things—the very land that had been the bone of contention between Church and State. First he had it under a temporary use permit, and then as an outright grant.

There had been one legal point to be cleared before the grant could be made: Did the Mission have a claim to this land through once having used it? A letter to Father Ramón Abella, by then in retirement at San Luís Obispo, took care of this. The Mission had used it, said Abella, and had resented its being taken by the Government, but had never had anything that could be called a title to it.

So, all investigations having been made and the deed of grant signed by the Governor, there remained only for this great day the final act of transmission, which was in itself an event worth describing—a formality rooted in ancient custom. The act was usually called "the survey" but it was not a job for engineers. It was a neighborhood affair—a viewing of the landmarks by all who might be concerned with the boundaries of the property being granted.

Everybody who might have an interest in the matter joined the group and in the presence of the local alcalde ·and impartial witnesses, all traveled around the property, noted the hills, rocks, trees, and valleys that marked its boundaries, and there agreed or voiced their protest. And as they went they measured the distance in *varas* to verify the number of square leagues it contained.

For this occasion the mounted group assembled at Point San Bruno on the Bay shore, at the northerly border of the modern city of South San Francisco. First a rawhide *cordel* or a lariat was stretched and measured, fifty Castilian *varas* in length, according to legal Mexican standards. Then the trip began.

The alcalde, who in this case happened to be Francisco de Haro, Sánchez' son-in-law, produced a pocket compass which he placed on an Indian shell mound and indicated a line to the west and northwest that should be the northern boundary of the rancho. But this line would take the party up over the highest and steepest hill in the San Bruno Mountains. To climb this seemed like a terrible waste of energy when the distance around it couldn't be very different from the distance over it. So, with Sánchez's consent, they took the more circuitous route through Paradise Valley. Anyway, what was a hillside among friends?

They could not know, of course, that twenty-five years later, with the country taken over by a bothersomely exacting lot of people, their failure to climb the hill would cause a prolonged legal dispute, and that all the survivors of this group would then be brought into court in an effort to determine whether they considered the line to be where they went, or over the hill where they did not go. Perhaps some of them were surprised when the court decided for them that the line was intended to be where they actually went—around the hill and not over it.

They were also quizzed, to their embarrassment, about their method of measuring. Having by then seen men with transits and chains measuring land by feet and inches, they were asked whether in their surveying they traveled on foot or horseback. At least one man insisted that they went on foot. Another said, "Some of it we measured on foot but sometimes we got tired and mounted our horses." How long did it take them this way to get around the rancho? Well, they started in the morning and finished shortly after noon. The distance is approximately twenty-five miles!

The usual procedure was for two mounted men to take the two ends of the *cordel,* approximately fifty yards long. The man ahead would then wait while the man behind him galloped past, measuring a hundred yards, then the latter, in turn, would wait while the other passed, and so on.

Traveling in this way, the party followed the route of the present Foothill Boulevard to what is now the first corner of Olivet Memorial Park. Here, all hands agreed, was Sánchez's corner, already marked by a pile of rocks. Here again the alcalde produced his compass and indicated a line running southwesterly across the valley. A horseman was sent ahead to locate Laguna Alta, just over the ridge, and to stand as a marker for them. The line was run over the hill and past the south end of this little lake at the junction of California Highway No. 1 with the Skyline Boulevard, but now no longer in existence, to a place overlooking the sea and "at the point of a canyon looking toward the coast of San Pedro and on the road thither." This again was Sánchez's corner and he agreed to mark it.

From here, the western boundary was measured, first aiming for the San Andreas Valley and then following the bottom of it to a point where there was "an ash tree on their right and a protruding rock on their left", and this was the southwest corner, today just north of the Spring Valley Lakes. Over the hill to the northeastward now, coming out on the Bay Shore, "passing the line by the edge of a small lagoon and just north of a small round hill". The lagoon has since been filled but its site is marked by Laguna Avenue in Burlingame, and the hill by Edgehill Drive. From here the party skirted the edge of the salt marsh, which kept them most of the way close to the present El Caminio Real and San Bruno's San Mateo Avenue, back to the point of beginning.

The measuring was done—a tract of four square leagues (15,000 acres) had been surveyed in a day. But there was still an important act to be put into the record, to symbolize the transfer of ownership. The sober official language of the document bears witness to the fact that the "said citizen José Sánchez pulled up grass and stones from the ground and threw them to the four winds as a sign of his legal and juridical possession" of the land. It was now his to do with as his fancy might dictate.

Yet this last was not quite true. There were, in fact, strings attached to insure that this would be a homestead and not merely a speculation. The land must not be sold, mortgaged, or entailed; trees must be planted, and within a year a house must

The original Charles Brown adobe, center above, still stands in
Woodside, remodeled.

The José Sánchez Buri-Buri home, sketched seven years after his
death, stood east of El Camino Real on the Burlingame-Millbrae
line.

be built and it must be inhabited. These were the usual requirements written into Mexican grants but it is doubtful whether any of them were ever seriously enforced.

Sánchez did build his house by the roadside where today the cities of Burlingame and Millbrae meet, and there he spent the remaining seven years of his life. On a near-by slough, or arm of the Bay, he built his *embarcadero,* or boat landing, for the shipment of his hides and tallow. According to his own report, he already had 2,000 head of cattle and 250 horses, and with the years the number increased.

Unlike many of the rancheros, Sánchez also farmed. Old maps show in the sheltered valleys on his property fields of wheat, corn, and vegetables, and among his possessions was a grist mill—all of which raised his holdings from the category of a mere rancho to that of an *hacienda.* Whether "raised" is the proper word might be disputed, however, for many of the wealthy *rancheros* considered farming beneath their dignity. Handling cattle could be the work of a gentleman, in the social code of the times, while farming was mere drudgery.

Not that the master of the ranch did either himself, though he might ride with the herd at the annual *rodeo* to see that his interests were protected, and perhaps on occasion show his skill with a rope. But he never would stoop to such menial tasks as driving an ox team. Laborers, mainly Indians held under a feudal-type attachment to the place, did his work with a few of the ablest and most favored peons being permitted to become vaqueros. This old social hierarchy, borrowed from feudal Europe and established in mission days, tended to prolong itself; Indians, even the most trusted neophytes, did not ride horseback except by special permission granted only to a favored few.

This land-granting process, during the decade that followed, was repeated many times over until all of the Peninsula's choicest land passed into private hands. To the west of Buri Buri, *San Pedro,* the cradle of mission work down the Peninsula, was acquired by Sánchez's son, Francisco, and where the ruins of the mission outpost still stood, he built his home, probably utilizing the same adobe bricks that the Mission converts had made there before he was born. His land, which reached over the ridge to join that of his father, turned out, when American engineers surveyed it, to cover 8,926 acres embracing approximately what is now the City of Pacifica; and his house, the Sánchez Adobe, still stands as a restored monument for today's generation to see.

To the north of Buri Buri lay the Lake Merced area and the San Bruno Mountains. The former was granted (1835) to one José Antonio Galindo but was bought two years later by Sánchez's son-in-law, Francisco de Haro, the alcalde who had presided at the old man's survey. For some reason, perhaps Galindo lacked influential friends, this grant was almost insultingly small—only one-half a square league, or 2,200 acres, including the lake. A portion of it is now in San Francisco.

The mountain area was granted to an American-turned-Mexican, Jacob Leese, who had married a sister of General Mariano Guadalupe Vallejo. He gave his land a name distinguished for its length—*Guadalupe La Visitacion y Rodeo Viejo*—but there was a reason for this; it left no room for questions as to what land was included. Guadalupe was the valley now marked by the town of Brisbane, named to show that the grant reached down to the Bay shore. La Visitacion defined its northerly extent, beyond the present Cow Palace, now in Visitacion Valley, while the scene of the "old Rodeo" (*Rodeo Viejo*) took it over the hill to the present Mission Street. Called two square leagues, it surveyed out at 9,500 acres.

To the south of Buri Buri was the tract called San Mateo, a square league in size. The mission outpost building and the dwindling remnant of the Mission's one-time neophytes were still on it, and, allegedly for this reason, it remained ungranted up to the very verge of the American occupation. Then Governor Pio Pico used it to pay a debt to a friend in Los Angeles. Cayetano Arenas, the grantee, frightened because the American invasion was already on, sold it to Mellus and Howard in San Francisco. In the 1850's William D. M. Howard made of it the first fancy stock farm in the San Francisco environs, and built on it the first country mansion down the Peninsula.

The land from San Mateo Creek to San Francisquito Creek at Palo Alto was one huge grant, by far the largest on the Peninsula, called *Rancho de las Pulgas*. Supposedly four square leagues, it turned out—when all the boundary disputes were settled—to be 35,250 acres. Its peculiar name, which means Ranch of the Fleas, whether or not this was actually its origin, memorialized the uncomfortable night of Portolá's soldiers in some flea-ridden Indian huts.

This tract was claimed by the Argüello family as having been granted to them under two different kings of Spain, but they had no documents to prove it. Title was actually acquired under a Mexican grant in 1835 to the widow and children of the former Governor Luís Argüello. The widow lived on it for a while and Luís may have spent some time there, though the only buildings were a *palizada* hut, the site of which is now in San Carlos, and a frame-and-mud structure in the Menlo Park area.

Stretching the length of the Peninsula's central valley, now the scene of wooded homesites and a chain of lakes, were three grants. Most northerly was *Rancho Feliz,* bordering Rancho San Mateo at the valley bottom and reaching to the top of the western ridge. The grantee, Domingo Feliz, was a grandson of José Sánchez.

To the south of this, and bordering Las Pulgas along the present Cañada Road, was *Rancho Cañada Raymundo* which took in the mountainside up to the Skyline Boulevard. This was granted to the well-known Englishman, John Coppinger, a personal friend and political supporter of Governor Juan B. Alvarado. Coppinger was a deserter from the British Navy who hid out in the Woodside redwoods and built the first substantial dwelling there, at the corner of the present Woodside and King's Mountain roads. He died in 1847 and his widow, Luisa Soto, later married John Greer.

Bordering Coppinger's land at Searsville, and lying partly in what is now Portola Valley, was *Rancho Corte de Madera,* so named because this was where timber was obtained. The land, about half of which lay in Santa Clara County, was granted jointly to Domingo Peralta of Oakland, and Máximo Martínez, who was a soldier of Spain as early as 1812, and who lived through the Mexican regime to become well-known in American times.

Turning finally to the Coastside, the rolling slopes between the mountains and the sea could not fail to attract cattle men. The stretch of land near Pillar Point had somehow become *El Corral de Tierra,* perhaps because the hills seemed to encircle it to form a great natural corral of earth, or perhaps more likely, the Point itself was used as a corral by simply fencing off its narrow neck.

This land was granted in two parts, each one a square league; the northerly half went to Francisco Guerrero Palomares, and the southerly portion, reaching to Pilarcitos Creek at the present town of Half Moon Bay, to Tiburcio Vásquez, cousin of the bandit of the same name. The line between the two was the creek at Miramar that still bears its old Spanish name, *El Arroyo de en Medio.* The tell-tale name indicates that at this creek, "in the middle" of the area, the cattle were rounded up for the annual rodeo.

South of Pilarcitos Creek was the Miramontes land, another square league. It was Candelario Miramontes who at first lived and grew potatoes where Portsmouth Square in San Francisco now is, and who petitioned for a larger grant because he had so "long" a family—*tan larga*—viz. thirteen children, that he had no place to put them. He moved to the present site of Half Moon Bay, and a little later, just across the creek northward from him lived Vásquez with his family of almost equal "length". The two families, with their in-laws and friends, formed the nucleus of a village called San Benito, which the American settlers dubbed Spanish-town.

Miramontes' neighbor on the south, who was not a very good neighbor, was one of the Alviso brothers who had another grant at Alviso south of the Bay. Miramontes complained that the Alvisos laid claim to land that was rightfully his and drove his men off whenever he tried to work it. Because of this quarrel there was a strip, a no-man's land, between them that neither was able to get title to. But on the south the Alvisos were more successful with their aggressive tactics. They got the land to Tunitas Creek although their first boundary was placed short of that stream at Lobitos Creek.

Next in line was *Rancho San Gregorio,* centering in the beautiful valley of San Gregorio Creek, and taking in four square leagues (17,783 acres) of grassy hills and wooded valleys. It belonged to Antonino Buelna of San José and Monterey, who was influential enough to get another land grant at the same time on the present site of Stanford University campus. He is said to have opened the first road over the mountains in this area. His southern boundary was Pomponio Creek.

This southerly land was held to be in the territory of Santa Cruz Mission, and under the American regime it was originally in Santa Cruz County. The grantee of *Rancho El Pescadero* was Juan José Gonzáles, *mayordomo,* or foreman, at the Santa Cruz Mission, and the padres there helped him, when secularization came, to get his grant. His adobe home was near Pescadero Creek (the name suggests good fishing there) at the site of the present town of Pescadero.

The last two ranchos, the *Bútano* and the *Punta del Año Nuevo,* furnish an illustration of the geographical confusion that sometimes characterized these grants. The Bútano was one square league and the Año Nuevo four, but both were described as being bounded on the north by Bútano Creek, and on the west by the ocean. Simeon Castro, grantee of the Año Nuevo, died about the time the grant was completed, and the family later sold the property, probably without knowing of the

The Sánchez Adobe before restoration; north side above, south
side below.

Francisco Sánchez, José's son, built his home on the old mission outpost site in Pedro Valley — perhaps using the original adobe walls. Below, his house after restoration.

confusion. Under the American regime both titles were confirmed, thus giving two separate owners a valid title to the same land, since even American engineers were unable to resolve the conflict of claims. This would no doubt have been the cause of a prolonged law suit but for the fact that one man, Loren Coburn, bought both claims.

Life for the rancheros, owners of these grants, could be easy and carefree, for during most of the year there was not much to do. The cattle, always identifiable by their brands, ranged freely with little or no watching, and there were servants to do the drudgery. Usually a little wheat, beans, and corn were grown for home consumption, but cultivation was kept at a minimum. Aside from these small matters there was in a year's time only one big event, namely, the *rodeo* (ro-dáy-o) and the *matanza*.

The rodeo could be a joint affair between neighbors, or it could be held individually on each rancho, but in either case the neighbors were all there. The cattle were rounded up, the new calves identified by the cows that mothered them, and branded; in case of doubt, the ownership was decided by an impartial *juez de campo* or field judge. If the neighboring herds were mixed, each man's cattle were sorted by brands so the owner could determine the number to be butchered.

Then came the matanza or slaughtering. The actual killing was done by skilled vaqueros who might, for the sheer sport of it, despite long horns, cut the animals' throats from the saddle while on a dead run, or they could rope them and then cut the jugular vein. The carcasses were left where they fell for the crew of skinners, and the men who cut off the fat portions to be cooked down as tallow.

Tallow bags were made by tying the edges of an undried hide to the tops of stakes driven into the ground, thus forming a large bowl into which the hot melted tallow was poured. Then, as it cooled and congealed, the edges of the hide were wrapped together and the whole tied in a bundle. This job had its hazards, for grizzly bears liked this tallow and if they happened to find it at the right consistency, i.e. still liquid but not too hot, they would drink the entire contents of the bag. Hence the workers kept a wary eye out and never stayed too late in the afternoon.

The skins to be sold were staked out to dry, to prevent curling, and the remaining carcasses were left for the dogs and coyotes. The dried hides and bundles of tallow were taken away to market in ox carts or on the backs of pack animals.

This was the year's harvest, which probably was already bargained for by the agents of ships from around the Horn. In fact rancheros were, in many instances, in debt a year or two in advance for goods bought and delivered on credit. Yet they were always regarded as good risks although they kept their accounts only by memory. In the Bay Area, William Richardson ran a lighterage business at Yerba Buena, now downtown San Francisco, collecting the hides and tallow at boat landings around the Bay and delivering them to ships in the harbor.

Some of these ranchero families, e.g. the Argüellos, were people of means and distinction who lived at the Presidio or in the village that had grown up around Mission Dolores, or perhaps in Monterey or San José. They kept their herdsmen on the rancho and probably came themselves only for the occasion of the rodeo. Others preferred to make their homes on the rancho. Such men built substantial adobe-brick houses and, by standards of the time, lived comfortably. An adobe house with a dirt floor could be made an attractive home, kept clean and decorated with growing flowers and climbing vines. On the other hand, it could be quite the opposite, and some undoubtedly were.

Most of the families took great pleasure in frequent dances and *meriendas* (picnics), which were indulged in at the slightest provocation, and especially at the rodeos. While the rodeo was a matter of serious business, the fact that it brought the neighbors together made it, of necessity, a social event. During the day there was always time for games and contests of skill in horsemanship, and at night a continuous round of feasting and dancing.

A favorite game was *correr al gallo,* in which a live rooster was buried with his neck and head protruding from the ground. Men on their horses galloped by at full speed and each tried, in turn, to seize the rooster by the neck and carry him away. Another competition involved mounted men who were handed trays of wine glasses, filled to the brim, which they were supposed to carry a given distance at a full gallop, then brake to a stop without spilling the wine.

Life on the whole was leisurely and simple; the people were neighborly and generous. The working servants were under a kind of peonage but laborers were too scarce to make likely any very serious abuses of their status. Nobody had much money, but the rancheros were, by their standards, wealthy. Money served mainly as a measuring device, and very little of it ever changed hands.

José Sánchez wrote in his will that he had in his chest "thirty *pesos* in silver and twenty-nine ounces of gold", but the debts that he owed and those that were owed to him were all in terms of barter. "Juan Copingea" (John Coppinger), he said, owed him "16 pesos which he received in soap, to be repaid in silver or hides"; Don Diego Escott" (James Scott) owed him 16 *pesos* in goods, Carlos Moreno (Charles Brown) 6 cow hides", and so on. To "Don Enrique Mellis" (Henry Mellus) he owed "228 pesos in produce, Sr. Tompson (probably Alpheas B. Thompson) 15 pesos in produce, and to Tiburcio Vásquez twenty-one calves." And one "Jorge Foqueson" (George Ferguson) had an unfinished contract to do some work on his house.

Probably there can be no sharper insight into the standards and customs of the times than is given in Sánchez's order regarding "Don Juan Yon" (John Jones). Mr. Jones, who was United States Consul at the time in Hawaii, owed him 1,108 pesos, he said, and through "Don Tomas Shoa" (Thomas Shaw), Jones had sent him 66 pesos on account of interest. "When he pays the principal," said Sánchez, "return to him the interest"! In his world lending money had nothing to do with business; it was a helping hand extended to one who was in trouble, and for this he could never stoop so low as to accept compensation.

But this idyllic world of the rancheros was short lived. For a brief decade it flourished, and Sánchez gives us in his will, all unconsciously, signs of its coming demise. All but one of the men named in connection with his business dealings were foreigners. The number of these in the country, mainly Americans, was constantly increasing. Sánchez died within a year (1843), and he was not dead more than three years when his children saw American soldiers on the march. The Mexican flag

The Coppinger-Greer adobe, built in 1841 by John Coppinger at Old County and King's Mountain roads, Woodside.

A hut for herdsmen on Rancho de las Pulgas, built before 1846, stood in Menlo Park until 1956, when John Wickett, to save it from destruction, moved it to King's Mountaintop!

was pulled down at Monterey, San Francisco, and San José, and the Stars and Stripes were put up in its place.

The "Americanizing" of California, viewed from the standpoint of the rancheros, may at first have been taken as a minor incident that sooner or later was bound to occur, but before long it became to them a major upheaval. The Sánchez family is a good example; if not typical, they were at least, by no means a rare or extreme case. The transfer of sovereignty from Mexico to the United States found them comfortably well-off and apparently secure in that position, but fifteen years later most of them were landless and poor. And this despite the fact that the Treaty of Guadalupe Hidalgo specifically guaranteed the rights of California property owners under the American flag.

How could a thing like this happen? To understand the answer we must turn for a short look into United States history.

At the same time that California men were asserting the rights of individual citizens to own land, against the monopoly of Church and State, in the great Mississippi Valley the Daniel Boones and Davy Crocketts were demanding the right to hold small, choice pieces of land they found on remote inland streams, basing their claims not on purchase or government grant but on prior possession.

The bitter complaint of the American squatter was that after he had pioneered in the wilderness, far ahead of the government surveyors (hence where the land was not yet for sale), and had there, with his bare hands, cleared the timber, built his home, and planted his crops, he was often cheated out of his legitimate gain. Speculators, perhaps in league with government politicians, could buy his land from under him and force him, after years of work, either to get off or to pay for the improvements he himself had made.

These squatters, whose name was legion and who carried the sympathy of all the "little" men everywhere, had waged a years-long fight for a pre-emption law that would legalize squatters' rights. Finally, in 1841, Congress had done it—passed a law permitting any frontier settler to file a claim to not more than 160 acres of un-surveyed government land, which would give him first right to purchase the claimed land when it went on the market. This was now a legal routine, but in many minds "squatters' rights" were something sacred, and the term carried an even broader meaning best expressed by the old saying "possession is nine-tenths of the law".

The American land-use pattern in all this had come to be, both in thinking and in practice, the small, one-man farm, lived on and worked by the owner. And the land-for-everybody idea was soon to find its ultimate expression in the homestead law, based on another slogan, "Uncle Sam is rich enough to GIVE us all a farm."

When Uncle Sam acquired California, and his nephews by the thousands came rushing in after gold, this pattern, in their minds, was the American way of life. Many of them soon tired of digging for gold and looked around for land on which to settle. But when they inquired, they were told, again and again, that this or that attractive land, stretching away as far as they could see, all belonged to *Don Fulano de Tal* who lived over there in the adobe house, or was nobody-knew-where.

The reaction to this was bound to be hostile. Something was wrong here, and the American way was to do something about it. Many of them squatted on private property as if it were government land, but more significant than this was the fact that political leaders sensed the hostility of Americans toward the California rancheros and capitalized on it. The great test came in the kind of process that would be set up to legalize Mexican land titles under the American system.

Two different approaches to the matter were considered in Congress: one, to devise a simple process of registering Mexican deeds under American law—assuming the titles to be valid unless proved otherwise; the other, to create a United States Land Commission to investigate *all* titles, putting the burden of proof on the ones who claimed ownership. The fact that some claims of ownership were known to be fraudulent played into the hands of the advocates of the latter plan, i.e.—men who were already conscious of the large "squatter vote" in California,—and their proposal was adopted.

Not only this, but as time went on the squatter influence grew stronger and even captivated the office of the United States Attorney General, with the result that his Department took the extreme position of assuming that *all* California titles were spurious. All of them, one by one, were fought in the courts, even those that had won the approval of the United States Land Commission.

This automatically saddled everyone who owned land in California, and wanted to keep it, with a heavy burden of litigation. He must appear with attorney and witnesses before the Land Commission, and even if successful there must repeat the process in court— just to establish his ownership.

In addition, there was the matter of boundaries. What with every piece of property identified only by hills and creeks, or "an ash tree and a protruding rock", each had to be surveyed under the direction of the United States Surveyor General, and the survey must be approved by the court. The Buri Buri case, settling whether the line went around the hill or over it, was only one in hundreds of such disputes, many of them fought bitterly by opposing claimants. There were appeals and counter appeals, involving both titles and boundaries, and a large percentage of these cases were carried even to the United States Supreme Court.

The rancheros, land-rich but money-poor, were caught in a fatal trap, between the United States Government on the one hand, and on the other a horde of unscrupulous lawyers and money lenders who were out to fleece everyone who could not defend himself. Recalling the man who ordered that interest paid to him be refunded, we find his sons *borrowing* money for court expenses at the going rate of three percent a month, compounded monthly. Such interest they of course could not pay, so the principal soon doubled and trebled, and, shortly, they had no land.

In many instances, probably most of them, the men who, after years of litigation, came out owning the land were not heirs of the original grantees but investors and speculators who had picked it up on a foreclosure or sheriff's sale. Rancho Buri Buri, for instance, was finally divided among some fifty owners, and a scant five percent of it was held by Sánchez heirs.

The Argüellos were fortunate in finding a sharp Spanish attorney, S. M. Mezes, who took over their troubles for a generous share of their Pulgas estate. Given the size of their grant, they could afford him, but they also needed him, for at the beginning of the legal process a rumor got out to the effect that the Pulgas title would not be approved by the Land Commission. As a result, the place was seeded down with squatters, each hoping to pre-empt some of it in case it should turn out to be government land. And of course during the years that the title was in litigation there was not much the owners could do about it.

In the County Assessor's book of 1853 there appear seventeen names of tax payers on Pulgas property with assessments like this one: "Real estate none, house and improvements, $300"! Five more, probably living in tents, were assessed for cattle, horses, oxen, etc., but no house. On the other hand, one W. C. R. Smith squatted in style with a "large, two-story house on the north side of Redwood Landing", but no real estate. In short, Redwood City got its start as a squatters' town. It would be interesting to know just how each one of the settlers fought it out with Mezes and how long it took to get all of the cases settled.

In many instances, innocent purchasers who acted in good faith were the worst sufferers; like Dennis Martin, who was the real victim in the celebrated Pulgas boundary dispute—one of the longest and most talked about in California. Martin bought land that both he and the seller believed to be part of Rancho Cañada Raymundo. He operated two saw mills, built a house and planted orchards, even built a chapel for public worship and set aside land for a cemetery. But the land he had bought was finally found by the court to be part of the Pulgas, and not Cañada Raymundo. The blow forced him into bankruptcy and he spent the rest of his life as a common laborer.

Stories could be multiplied almost without limit to illustrate the confusion and uncertainty of land titles, many of them tragic, some fantastic, some amusing. For just one more, there is the twisted tale of the Julia Sánchez de Valencia family, headed by one of José Sánchez's five daughters. Julia died before this trouble began, leaving a husband who was alleged to be incompetent, and some children. A real estate and "legal" firm known as Wainwright, Randall & Co., managed to get Randall appointed guardian of the father and children, and administrator of Julia's estate, consisting of some 1,500 acres of land, which was her undivided share of Rancho Buri Buri.

Randall's first move was to ask the court's permission to sell the property, since the land was unproductive and the family needed money. Permission was granted, the land was officially appraised at $10.00 an acre, but sold at public auction for $7.50 an acre, cash on the barrel head, to one Charles Gulliver.

Some years later, Randall, in an administrator's report to the court, showed expenditures for the family amounting to something over $7,400, and for "expenses of administration", $3,214.95. Out of some $12,000 received from the original sale and accumulated interest, there remained to the credit of the estate about $1,500.

But this was not the end. San Francisco courts were swarming with brilliant attorneys watching for opportunities of this kind, and one of them came forward with the idea that since the State of California did not come into being until after Julia's death, it had no jurisdiction over her estate, and this whole process from

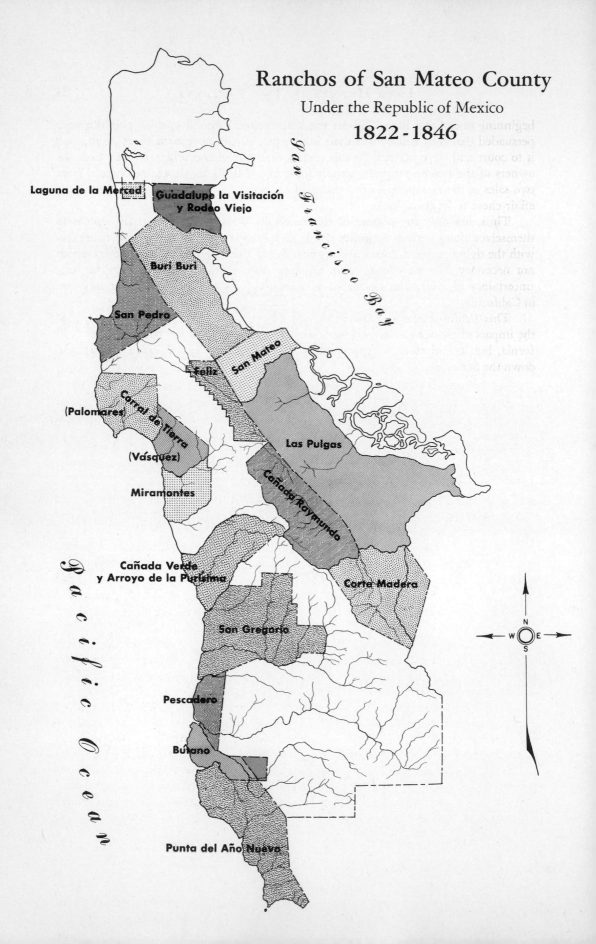

# Ranchos of San Mateo County

Under the Republic of Mexico

## 1822-1846

Laguna de la Merced

Guadalupe la Visitación
y Rodeo Viejo

Buri Buri

San Pedro

Feliz    San Mateo

(Palomares)    Corral de Tierra

(Vásquez)    Las Pulgas

Miramontes

Cañada Raymunda

Cañada Verde
y Arroyo de la Purísima    Corta Madera

San Gregorio

Pescadero

Bútano

Punta del Año Nueva

*San Francisco Bay*

*Pacific Ocean*

N
W · E
S

beginning to end was illegal. Under this assumption, Valencia and his children were persuaded that they still owned their land, other parties purchased their claim, took it to court and were upheld! In this case, which was of course a rare exception, the owners of the rancho property, simply by doing nothing at all, enjoyed profit from two sales of their property—or as much of it, that is, as the real manipulators of the affair chose to let them have.

Thus, not only the regime of the rancheros was liquidated but the rancheros themselves along with it. Regimes die as new ones come into being, and inevitably with the dying go pains, losses and regrets. But in this case most of the suffering was not necessary. Not only was grave injustice done to the rancheros, but the long uncertainty of land titles became a serious brake on the growth of the new era in California.

This Peninsula, being close to the center of things in the Gold Rush era, felt the impact of change sooner and more violently than some of the other parts of California, but its sad story is typical of what was repeated again and again up and down the State.

Timothy Guy Phelps, Gold Rusher Extraordinary.

# IV. The Gold Rush: *Those who came to stay*

*"The miners themselves were the least likely of all men in California
to become wealthy."*                                        Josiah Royce

Early in the summer of the magic year of 1849, some young men were sitting in
a San Francisco boarding house making plans for a trip—not to the gold fields, but
southward to the redwood forest, only some thirty miles away.

Building materials, they noted, were commanding fantastic prices. Only since
the first of the year many thousands of people had settled in San Francisco and were
living precariously in a mass of tents and shacks that filled the water front and was
climbing up the hillsides.

M. A. Parkhurst, his friend Ellis, and perhaps others, had decided that the City's
booming market, plus these near-by redwoods, offered greater inducements than
digging for elusive gold. Sawmills were rare and expensive, but they could make
shingles; for this operation one needed only a pack-horse or mule, a few tools, camp-
ing equipment, and a grubstake.

While outfitting themselves for their safari, they met a dentist from New
England who had come to practice his profession in San Francisco, but who was
sick and unhappy. First he had become disgusted with things in the wild city and
decided to go to the mines. He was charging four dollars per tooth for extractions,
and his strong sense of fair dealing kept him from putting his price any higher, but
his friend and competitor was collecting four times that amount, using the simple
formula, "an ounce for a tooth".

But the dentist-with-a-conscience, whose name was Robert Orville Tripp, had
the bad luck to be shipwrecked on his way up the river; he got thoroughly soaked in
the cold water and came back seriously ill. When Parkhurst and Ellis invited him to
come and recuperate in their Woodside sunshine, he accepted. The result was that
he stayed there the rest of his life, which turned out to be almost sixty years.

The account of his trip down the Peninsula, in mid-summer, 1849, is revealing.
There was as yet no stagecoach service, so, to avoid crossing the sand dunes, he took
a sail boat from the San Francisco water front to Mission Slough. From the mission
he walked to the *portezuela* (Daly City's gap in the hill), sat down to rest, and
noted, as he surveyed the landscape, that there was not a building in sight.

But a man came by with a wagon and offered him a ride (for five dollars) to the Sánchez Ranch (Millbrae), where they both stayed for the night. Next day, the same man hauled him to his destination—for ten dollars. But to reach the redwoods, the only known route was the circuitous one of traveling southward to the site of Palo Alto, then following San Francisquito Creek to the Mountain Home Ranch, which was Charles Brown's Adobe, in the Woodside valley.

Dr. Tripp soon found his friends, Parkhurst and Ellis, but he didn't work with them in making shingles—at least not for long; what he planned was something bigger than shakes. In San Francisco a fever of wharf-building started early in 1850; Tripp and others foresaw this need and prepared to supply the necessary timber. Tripp and Parkhurst formed a partnership with some San Francisco builders—a man named Ryder, later known as Grizzly Ryder, because of a celebrated encounter with a bear, a Mr. Hayward, and a Mr. Lloyd, probably William, who later had a blacksmith shop in Searsville.

These three came down by boat to view the situation, and in so doing made a lucky mistake. In taking, as they thought, the regular route up San Francisquito Creek, they found on arrival that they had come up Redwood Creek instead and had discovered a much shorter route. The partners then proceeded to open a direct road from the redwoods to the head of tidewater in Redwood Slough or Creek. Thus this spot came, in time, to be the heart of Redwood City.

Using oxen for power, they dragged their hand-squared timbers and round logs to the bank of the slough, piling them at a spot that is now back of the buildings on the northwest corner of Broadway and Main Street. When enough had been accumulated, they were rolled into the water, tied together in rafts, and at the moment of the outward-turning tide, were started on their winding journey down the slough to the Bay, and on with the tide as it moved to the Golden Gate. When the tide turned, the pilot simply dropped an anchor and waited for the next ebb tide. A hitch or two like this, and a short tow into the cove at San Francisco, and the timber had reached its market.

In this way Dr. Tripp and his partner became unwittingly the founders of Redwood City. If the "slough" was good or floating logs, it could also carry schooner-loads of lumber. When this was proved to be true, the next step was to build more schooners, and to do it conveniently on the banks of the same slough. These activities required dwellings, stores, and blacksmith shops, which soon constituted a town.

But Tripp, meanwhile, had turned to something else. Seeing among the redwoods a growing number of sawmill men, wood choppers, shingle makers and "bull-whackers", he and his friend Parkhurst built a shack and put out a sign, "Woodside Store". This was in 1851. By 1854 they had built a better building—the one that still stands, across the road from the first one. Parkhurst died in 1863, though only 34 years of age, but Tripp stayed on in business in the same building until the time of his death, on the last day of March, 1909.

Dr. Tripp had many stories to tell about his early pioneering. His store, when he first opened it, was the only one between San Francisco and Santa Clara. His first merchandise was freighted by wagon from San Francisco, but he soon began using a flat-bottomed boat. He sent a man with a wagon to meet his first boatload that came up Redwood Slough, but the man hunted all day and could not find it. Tripp finally had to go after it himself, but he also had to pay the man $25.00 for his time spent hunting for it. He sold goods and supplies for the first store in Pescadero, which were carried over the mountain on pack mules. His own customers came from as far away as San Mateo and Half Moon Bay.

Dr. Tripp had no political ambitions, nevertheless in 1851 he received notice that he was running for supervisor in San Francisco County (which then included most of the Peninsula). He was elected, and for some time thereafter rode a horse to the City every Sunday for the Board meeting on Monday.

As country dentist and storekeeper, Tripp made a deep mark on Woodside, and his name became known everywhere on the Peninsula. He was considered a good dentist, when even bad ones were hard to come by, and he kept a good store— aiming to have on hand in his small building almost every kind of staple goods the people might need. When getting-around was limited to horse travel, this was important.

In those times, country stores were everywhere, something like filling stations today, but rarely did a storekeeper become a phenomenon in his community as did Dr. Tripp. He did nothing in particular to achieve this distinction except to stick quietly to his business and his profession, but in so doing he sooner or later came to know, almost intimately, every family in his valley and up on the mountain. His meticulously-kept ledger carried accounts with most of them, so he knew their financial rating, what foods and patent medicines they bought, and what they drank, if any; he pulled and "plugged" their teeth, handled their mail, and probably heard all the gossip about them, though he himself was not a gossip-monger. They, on the other hand, respected his fine sensibilities, his gentlemanly personality, and, of course, his integrity.

A final reason why he became the symbol of an era in Peninsula history was his own durability. Woodside changed with the years, one generation passed and another came on, but he seemed to go on forever. When finally his end came, his store was closed; time had passed it by and its location was no longer a good business spot. But still it stood, the stark expression of his well known personality; and so, though closed and its windows barred, it became a community shrine long before it was purchased by the County and made a public museum.

Woodside was by no means the only American-type community on the Peninsula, but it was the earliest and for a time the busiest. Ten years after Tripp's arrival, the editor of the San Mateo County *Gazette* tried to describe the place and apparently found the task a bit difficult. He had just founded the Peninsula's first newspaper (1859) and was describing the various parts of the county as he found them.

"Woodside", he wrote, " - - - - - though it makes no pretention to the title of town or village, is nevertheless somewhat of a public place. Situated at the foot of the mountains, in the immediate vicinity of several (saw) mills, it is the center of quite a trade. It has one store in which is the post-office. Mountain Dell Division No. 74, Sons of Temperance, is located here. At this point, also, the citizens have done what has not been accomplished in any other place in the county—they have formed

LUMBERING was San Mateo County's first industry. Dragging logs to the mill from steep and dusty mountain canyons was heavy work best done by steady, powerful oxen.

Steam sawmill near Pescadero.

Wagons had limited usefulness in mountainous country.

Redwood City lumber-shipping basin, photographed at low tide about 1865, was near Broadway and Main. The Congregational Church in the background was at Jefferson Avenue and Middlefield Road.

Dr. Tripp's Woodside Store, built in 1854.

Robert Orville Tripp was the first merchant and first dentist down the Peninsula. His store is now a historic shrine and county landmark.

a library association, and have already accumulated quite an extensive library of excellent works."

The "public place" of 1859 was mainly a product of the Gold Rush but it had an earlier history too. The Woodside-Searsville-Portola Valley had been tapped for timber in Spanish times by Mission Santa Clara and the town of San José, and by the mission and presidio of San Francisco. Then came the two land grants already mentioned, El Corte de Madera and Cañada Raymundo, on which there was more timber cutting, some cattle grazing and a little farming.

The valley had also served as a hideout for runaways. John Coppinger himself, grantee of Cañada Raymundo, was a deserter from the British Navy, and James Pease joined him after taking French leave of the Hudson's Bay Company ship *Neried* in San Francisco Bay. There were others also of uncertain background who congregated in the beautiful, secluded valley.

Coppinger built an adobe house (1841) at the corner of King's Mountain and Woodside roads which stood until the 1906 earthquake. Charles Brown who built the first sawmill also built the adobe that still stands, unofficially bearing his name.

During the late years of the Mexican regime, the number of foreigners in California, most of whom were Americans, increased rapidly; and a good many of them found their way into the "Pulgas Redwoods", as the Woodside Valley was then called, to work at whipsawing lumber. Just how many of them were there at any given time it is impossible to say, but beginning with "Bill the Sawyer" Smith, about fifty names can be accounted for, of men who were there and who stayed for at least a few months.

A sample of what was going on is offered by a receipt signed by Coppinger in 1834, well before there were any sawmills, for 3,350 feet of lumber. To turn out this quantity of sawed timber or planks would require a team of two men working steadily for about six weeks. It was done by rolling the log to be sawed over a long pit, where it rested on cross-logs and was ripped with a two-man saw, one man working on top of the log and the other beneath it.

A local folk tale, apropos the hugeness of the logs, told of a man below in such a pit who seemed to be getting little help from above; he crawled out of a cloud of sawdust to investigate and found his partner fast asleep on top of the log.

The first sawmills, when they came, were water-powered, with one straight saw working up and down on a crank. Later, steam was introduced, as well as "gang" mills, circular saws, and other improvements. By 1859, when the *Gazette* man visited this "public place", there were at least eight sawmills and three shingle mills working in the Woodside area, with a combined capacity of 56,000 board feet of lumber a day. Soon afterwards the mills were to begin moving up the canyons and over the mountain as the lower levels were timbered out.

This moving of the mills brought changes to the community, but the boom-town atmosphere of the early lumbering days was never quite rubbed out. Its early importance is pointed up by the fact that, from 1852, there was regular stage-coach service direct from Woodside to San Francisco and, from 1854, a post office, second in the county (after Steinberger's, which was later moved to Redwood City).

As early as 1851, there was a school house that served also as a "church and public hall". John Greer, who that same year married Coppinger's widow, gave the land, and by 1859 it enrolled 112 pupils. Another school to the northward, up West Union Creek where there were more sawmills, listed 72 pupils compared to Redwood City's 85.

The Sons of Temperance post impressed all observers as something remarkable for a lumberjack town. The secret of its success, however, was the fact that the meetings were held in the home of a widow with a very marriageable daughter—all this in the days when wives were so scarce as to justify almost any sacrifice—even abstinence—to acquire one. When the daughter announced her engagement (to a stranger from out of town!), it was said the temperance organization began to fall apart. On the widow we have no report.

The Library Association was a more serious affair and among the first in California. The members bought stock at five dollars a share and paid monthly dues of twenty-five cents. An initial purchase of 190 volumes was made, and later purchases brought the number up to 589. The book list also bespeaks an acquaintance with the world of literature. There was an active circulation for about five years from January, 1859; then it began to decline as the community became scattered with the moving of the mills. In 1872 the association was dissolved and the books distributed among the last remaining members. Meanwhile, at least three similar associations were organized, in Redwood City, San Mateo, and Pescadero.

The valley has undergone changes since then, from lumbering to farming, to country homes for the wealthy; but the people of Woodside are still deeply sentimental about those lumbering days, and the sentiment clings particularly about Dr. Tripp's old Woodside Store.

Many other young "men of forty-nine" were attracted, like Tripp and his friends, by the golden opportunities down the Peninsula. San Francisco's mushrooming population was demanding foodstuffs as well as lumber, so they hurried to buy, lease, or squat on the land and make it produce. The net result was that, within a decade, they had transformed much of the vacant cattle range, as well as the redwood forest, into an American community of farms, lumber camps and incipient villages.

While Dr. Tripp was building his store and beginning to forget that he was a sick man, Isaiah C. Woods, a person of quite different mold, was making plans and investments not far away, and modestly putting his name on the map in his port town of Raven*swood* and his nearby farm among the oaks of the present Menlo Park which he called *Wood*side Dairy.

He invested heavily in the twin ventures which, it seemed at the time, could not fail. Ravenswood occupied the one spot on all the south Bay shore where good land came close to deep water with no mud flats or winding sloughs, and near it was a vast area of potentially rich farming land, plus the lumber woods beyond—all of which, it seemed, would have to depend on this port for shipping.

He did not reckon with Dr. Tripp and the slough at Redwood City, but his real trouble was more immediate than that. Besides his Peninsula ventures, he was chief owner of Adams & Co. of San Francisco, in the business of banking and express service, and when California suffered its first financial panic (1855), he faced a crisis. In the absence of laws to protect depositors, as there are today, Woods sought only to protect himself. When his bank closed to prevent a run on its deposits, the remaining assets were secretly tranferred to the keeping of another firm, Palmer, Cook & Co., out of reach of the creditors.

But this was not all. In his maneuver, Woods planned a little scheme to salvage something for himself personally. Somehow he managed to sequester a considerable sum of gold which he took down the Peninsula and hid in the small frame-and-mud house that stood on his property.

But apparently somebody knew what was going on and whispered the secret to one Maurice Dooley, owner of a line of stagecoaches and a heavy depositor in the bank. Dooley also made his way down the Peninsula, faced Woods with a gun, and forced him thus to proceed to the hut where the gold was hidden and there count out to him enough to cover his balance in the bank—no more, no less. The sum, according to the late Moses Kavanagh, whose father was a friend of Dooley's and who exhibited the gun that did the trick, was eighty thousand dollars.

This little affair was known at the time to the two men involved and apparently no one else, but Woods was having plenty of trouble facing an angry public. He tried to calm his creditors with statements in the newspapers saying he was making every effort to raise funds to protect their interests, and finally he took passage on a ship just as a well-timed announcement appeared in the press assuring everyone that he was leaving for New York for this very unselfish purpose.

After this he seems never to have been seen or heard of in these parts, with but one exception: a man arrived from Hawaii who said he had seen Woods in Honolulu, a passenger on a ship bound for Australia. His tangible assets on the Peninsula were seized by the sheriff and sold at auction, including the land, dairy, and "lots in the town of Ravenswood".

Mr. Woods' dairy was only one among many on the Peninsula. Those nearest to San Francisco sold milk direct to the consumers, while those farther away, having no refrigeration, had to concentrate on making butter and cheese. The best cooling system known in those days was a stream of cold running water.

Where did the dairy cows come from? The first ones walked across the country in the wake of the Forty Niners, and they were often supplemented by a few "Spanish cattle". The Spanish Californians used little or no milk and ran mostly steers. Also they preferred their beef tough—it was "stronger" that way. Hence their longhorn cattle, raised mainly for the hides, were not much good by American standards, for either dairy or beef purposes. An item from the assessor's list of 1853 shows how they rated:

| | | |
|---|---|---|
| " 7 Spanish cows | $40. | $280. |
| 11 American " | 75. | 825." |

Some beginnings were small, like this farmer with 18 cows, while others were large investments like that of the Johnston brothers of the Coastside who, in 1853, drove a large herd from Ohio to California. In either case, the methods were the same in those unmechanized days. The cows were milked by hand, and the milk was either marketed at once, started on its way to becoming cheese, or set up in rows of shallow tin pans for the rising of the cream, which was then skimmed off and left to sour for churning into butter.

By 1860 the farms of San Mateo County were marketing more than 200,000 pounds of butter a year, and some 23,000 pounds of cheese. But farming was not limited to dairying, as is shown by the 1860 census which reported as one year's crop, 165,163 bushels of wheat, more than a hundred thousand of oats and barley, and 2,882 bushels of beans and peas, besides smaller quantities of corn, rice, and wool, not to mention mutton and pork. There were sold also some thousand gallons of wine, and $1,545 worth of fruit from orchards planted early in the decade.

One large-scale farmer and dairyman must be given special mention, not primarily as an agriculturist but because he became the Peninsula's most famous citizen—and many would say its finest: Timothy Guy Phelps. He was a Forty Niner at age 25 who tried and failed at mining but did well as a merchant in San Francisco. As a grain buyer, he learned about land down the Peninsula and, in 1853, began buying property where now stands the city of San Carlos, along the north bank of Cordilleras Creek. Ultimately, he had a farm of some 3,500 acres.

Except for his inherited personal talents, he was a completely self-made man. His father had suffered financial reverses, hence young Timothy's education, except for the rudiments taught in a village school, was all self-acquired. But he developed great power as a public speaker, served in the State Legislature and in Congress, became a personal friend of President Lincoln, and was twice a serious contender for the Governorship of California. He spent nineteen years as a member and Acting President of the Regents of the University of California, and served also on the Board of Lick Observatory.

Meanwhile on his dairy farm, until he sold it in 1887 to make way for a town of San Carlos, some 500 cows were milked regularly, and he frequently worked personally in the field with his men. As a capitalist, he invested in various California enterprises including mining, railroad building, and in the founding of the Peninsula's first financial institution, the Bank of Redwood City. Although he became a wealthy man, his interests and sympathies remained democratic. He died in 1899 as a result of a bizarre accident, being knocked down by two careless riders on a tandem bicycle.

Another heavy investor on the Peninsula, though not in dairying, was Charles Lux, owner of a large butchering business in San Francisco. He bought from Isidro Sánchez his entire one-tenth inheritance of Rancho Buri Buri (1,500 acres), which in time became the down-town portion of the city of South San Francisco. Here he built an elegant home, and it was here that he met Henry Miller, and the two laid the foundation of the famous California partnership of Miller and Lux. Thereafter Lux's farm became the assembling place for Miller & Lux cattle en route to the San Francisco market.

Later mention will be made of William D. M. Howard and his estate at San Mateo, and in beautiful Belmont Canyon three noteworthy men made their homes: S. M. Mezes, the attorney from Puerto Rico who handled the Argüello properties on Rancho de las Pulgas; ex-Governor John McDougal; and Count Leonetto Cipriani, an Italian who had business associations with Mezes. These few men were forerunners of many more who, a little later, would be building palatial homes down the Peninsula, primarily for no other reason than that it was a good place to live.

But wealthy men were by no means the only Peninsula developers; this fact was dramatically proved by an interesting series of events in the north end of the county.

There the stretch of rolling hills between two ranchos, Buri Buri on the south and Laguna de la Merced near the county line, was sold in small acreages by the United States Government, just as all government land was sold before the Homestead law was passed. Most of the buyers were young veterans of the Mexican War who used their war service bonus, which came then in the form of land bounty certificates, in part payment for tracts of 40, 60, or 160 acres, as they were able.

This land had been claimed by the grantees of Rancho Laguna de la Merced but the claim was denied and in 1853 the land was released for sale as U. S. Government property. During August and September of that year twenty-one settlers began improvements on their small farms, and simultaneously seventeen modest houses, all within sight of each other, were under construction.

When the rains came, the land blossomed with crops of potatoes and garden products, and for six years these young farmers went on developing their property. Then disaster fell. The first hint of it was the appearance of surveyors trampling through their crops. The latest owners of Rancho Laguna de la Merced (not the original grantees) had obtained a court order for another survey, in an attempt to get their grant relocated farther south. They would like to have it include some good land—not just sand dunes around the lake.

Efforts by the farmers to defend themselves in this unexpected crisis resulted only in bitter frustration, for nothing the settlers could do seemed to avail them anything. In desperation, they decided at one time to use some of their war experience in resisting eviction. They fortified a barn with bags of potatoes, set up a brass cannon, and prepared to defy the sheriff's posse. There was almost a Battle of Colma to go down in history. But the besieged were persuaded to abandon this tactic, and their redoubt as well. Instead, they organized the North San Mateo Settlers' Union and elected one of their number, R. S. Thornton, to conduct the necessary legal battle.

The case was carried even to the United States Supreme Court and Thornton spent most of the Civil War years in Washington, fighting his own war and that of his San Mateo neighbors. Finally, in May, 1866, he returned with victory for the settlers who were finally permitted to reoccupy their farms.

Where people go merchants follow, and the first merchandising institutions down the Peninsula sprang up late in 1849 along the old mission trail, soon to be called County Road, and later El Camino Real. Hitherto a mere dirt trail with no improvements, it had been traveled only by ox carts and men on horseback; now there were American wagons and stagecoaches, and even men on foot. A new State of

California was being organized and San José, only fifty miles from San Francisco, was slated to become the capital city.

To a certain Gold Rusher from New York named Nicholas de Peyster, the traffic along this road meant a business opportunity. He, by instinct and experience, was neither a farmer nor a miner; instead, merchandising was infused in his blood by his Hollander ancestors who had come to trade with the Indians at New Amsterdam on Manhattan Island. Finding the old mission adobe by San Mateo Creek standing empty and useless by the roadside, de Peyster and a partner cleaned it up and moved in with a stock of liquor and whatever merchandise they felt travelers might want, and opened what he called a "store and public house".

We have a report on the quality of de Peyster's brandy—not to mention San Mateo Milk—from one of his customers, another young Gold Rusher who wrote to his girl back home about his horseback ride to San José. At the old mission building by San Mateo Creek, he wrote, "We dismounted to take some refreshments and let our horses breathe. The (I blush a little) Milk Punch was excellent".

De Peyster's business prospered for more than a year. Henry Mellus, of the San Francisco firm of Mellus and Howard that had bought Rancho San Mateo, came by in a stagecoach and warned the merchants to get off his property. But they, like most squatters, paid no heed. However, in 1850 or 1851, de Peyster legally bought some 75 acres of Pulgas land across the creek, covering the area of San Mateo's present downtown business district, and there he built a hotel of his own.

His hostelry in time became famous as the San Mateo House, also known as the Half Way House (to San José). De Peyster sold out in 1856 and apparently returned to New York; but during his short stay south of San Francisco he had made history by establishing the first business enterprise in the town of San Mateo and by setting the location of that city's first business district. Meantime, he had served as the Peninsula's constable or deputy sheriff.

Soon there was a string of stopping places like de Peyster's along the road, all the way from San Francisco to San José. Some were farm houses where travelers were entertained as a side line; many carried some merchandise as well. They called themselves hotels, but in the beginning this only meant that the traveler could eat as well drink, and that he was welcome to stay overnight if he carried his own blankets and didn't mind sleeping in a haystack or under a tree. These rude inns soon developed better accommodations, however, and became regular stagecoach stops.

Traveling southward from San Francisco in the early 1850's, one encountered the first of these places where Daly City now stands. It was known as the Abbey House, though where it got its name is a puzzle; certainly it never showed any symptoms of being a religious center. It stood on the V-shaped point where Mission Street and San José Avenue meet—a spot that even in the ox-cart days had been a place of merging traffic, for here were then joined the southward trails from the Mission and the Presidio. The Abbey House was a landmark for more than half a century and was still there in 1906 when refugees from the earthquake and fire in San Francisco began forming the nucleus of a town to be called Daly City.

# Redwood City

San Mateo County July 7th 1856 First meeting of the Board of Supervisors after the organization of said County

The board of Supervisors of San Mateo County met this day at Redwood City present James Berry and Charles Clarke they constituting a majority of said board, duly organised for the transaction of business

The resignation of Horace Templeton as Majistrate having been previously handed in they proceeded to appoint a suitable person to fill the vacancy according to authority as provided by the Statutes. James McCrea was nominated and unanimously Elected to act as Justice of the Peace to fill said vacancy, and as a vacancy had occured in the Office of Constable by the resignation of J W Ackerson Mr Thomas H Beebe was duly appointed to fill said vacancy

And it further appearing that John N Reid is incompetent to fill the office of Majistrate which he now holds and in fact refuses to perform the duties of his office. On motion of Charles Clarke his office is declared vacated and David Marvin was duly appointed to the Office of Majistrate in place of said Reid. And it further appearing that a vacancy exists in that district in the Office of Constable Charles Shadick was duly appointed to fill said office of constable in said District

The board then proceded to consider the condition of the principal road through the county and unanimously decided that said road leading from San Francisco to Santa Clara must be repaired and on motion of James Berry. Charles Clarke was authorised to contract for repairs on said road at an expense not to Exceed fifty Dollars

The county Clerk Recorder and Treasurer having represented to the board that the Books Papers and Treasure of the county could

First county appropriation—$50 for roads . . .

The San Mateo House, now part of the Mills Memorial Hospital
nurses' home.

ROADHOUSES of stagecoach days, like motels of today, were
spaced at convenient intervals along El Camino Real. Some of the
memorable roadhouses were: The Abbey House in present Daly
City; the Twelve Mile House, still open in South San Francisco;
Fourteen Mile House, San Bruno; and the Seventeen Mile House at
Millbrae. The San Mateo House was the half-way stop for travelers
making the seven-hour trip to San José. An 1856 stage schedule
reads: "C. McLaughlin's daily line of Concord coaches leaves the
Plaza every morning (Sunday not excepted) at 8 for Redwood, San
Mateo, Santa Clara, and San Jose. Returning: Leaves San Jose every
morning at 7. The Company's coaches leave Oakland every day for
Union Springs, Mission of San Jose, Warm Springs and San Jose,
on arrival of the 10 a.m. boat from San Francisco . . ."

El Camino Real in 1850, as sketched by William H. Dougal. The view is from San Mateo, facing Belmont. In his scene below, near Menlo Park, C. A. Angelo offers roadside service in a tent.

The tank wagon, standing by the toll house on King's Mountain Road near the Woodside Store, was used frequently to help keep the dust down.

The survey crew (1911) for California's first state-financed highway project are seen working near San Bruno.

Ground-breaking ceremony for state highway work at San Bruno, 1912.

Next stop was the Twelve Mile House—the most durable one of all for it still sells liquor on the same spot (1963) and under the same name. Anyone interested, either in a drink or in history, will find it in South San Francisco, just off Grand Avenue on Old Mission Road—a short street that marks the old-time route of the highway.

This house and the next two stops performed for travelers one of the functions of modern automobile speedometers, that is, measuring the distance traveled. Next was the Fourteen Mile House and the other the Seventeen Mile House. The former, which stood where there are now two big supermarkets at the end of San Mateo Avenue in San Bruno, later became Thorp's Place and then Uncle Tom's Cabin— and it still carries on under the same name though in a new location. The Seventeen Mile House would now be on the northwest corner of Millbrae Avenue and El Camino Real.

After San Mateo came the Angelo House. Charles Aubrey Angelo, an Englishman in the Gold Rush, had first set himself up in business in a tent among the oaks in the present Menlo Park. Late in 1849 he was there with a sign on his tent, "Stage House", and apparently little else. Perhaps the stages wouldn't stop; at any rate sometime in 1850 he acquired land and put up a building farther north, at the entrance to the *Cañada del Diablo,* now Belmont. This spot made more sense,

70

business-wise, for it was the point where a major route took off through the canyon to the central valley and the Coastside. The place soon passed into other hands but as the Angelo House and as Flashner's it made considerable history.

The first hotel in Redwood City was the American House, on Main Street at Broadway, where at least there were bunks to sleep in though not in private rooms. At Five Points was the Pulgas House, whose name must not have been much of an asset, though perhaps appropriate; but most Gold Rush Americans didn't know enough Spanish to make it mean anything.

The final stop before reaching Santa Clara was Whistman's Ranch at Mountain View. This was mentioned by many travelers as a place of great relief to weary strangers for here was an American family, a good bed and good food.

In summarizing the changes that the first decade of American life brought to the Peninsula, we are helped enormously by Bayard Taylor, well-known in his day as a writer of travelogues, who made two revealing visits here—in 1849 and 1859. On his first trip, in the dry summer time while he was *walking* from San Francisco to Monterey to cover the California Constitutional Convention, he remembered mainly the "twenty miles without water", and that along the way through open country there was not much to mention other than the Sánchez Ranch (Millbrae) and the old mission adobe (San Mateo).

But just ten years later he grew eloquent over the changes he saw: the road was fenced, and "farm now succeeds farm, the whirling windmill beside each house, pumping up orchards and gardens to beautify the waste". The white farm houses, he thought were well placed in attractive spots under trees, and the architecture was well adapted to the scene—the roofs not so steep as in the East and often a veranda completely surrounding the house.

Such quick adaptation to California climate was not complete, of course; there were many houses, which he perhaps did not see, with roofs just as steep as if they were required to shed a heavy load of snow.

Taylor traveled along the County Road, now El Camino Real, but there was also a similar road running the length of the valley that was later usurped by the Crystal Spring Lakes. Along this, too, "farm succeeded to farm", from San Andreas on the north to the Woodside lumbering scene on the south, and near the present concrete dam, hidden deep in the valley, was a popular resort hotel called Crystal Springs. Likewise, down the Coastside from Montara to Pescadero, then in Santa Cruz County, there were at least 150 farms.

At San Mateo Taylor saw on his right as he traveled southward, this time (1859) by stagecoach, William D. M. Howard's "beautiful gothic residence" among the oak trees, and after crossing the creek on a good wooden bridge, he drew up on the left at a handsome hotel set in "neatness, comfort, and a profusion of shrubs, flowers, and vines". This, of course, was the San Mateo House, first owned by Nicholas de Peyster. Across from the hotel he visited the home of his friend, Fred Macondray, where he went into ecstacies over the fruit: "Such peaches, such pears, such apples and figs! What magic is there in this virgin soil?" But of San Mateo in 1859 this was all, except for a port at the mouth of the creek, and, shortly afterward, Henry Husing's store by the highway.

Redwood City, Taylor guessed, was a town of four or five hundred people, sitting out on the open plain, and ten miles beyond he could see the tall redwood tree, the landmark which the Spaniards had called the palo alto. Redwood City was the county seat, proud of its little two-story courthouse, just a year old, and busy building ships and shipping lumber.

Having started as a squatter settlement on Pulgas property, the town was already somewhat of a village when S. M. Mezes, agent for the rancho owners, had it surveyed and mapped (1854) and named it after himself, Mezesville. But no one seems to have taken the name seriously. Though not incorporated until 1867, it was commonly called Redwood Landing or Redwood City, and the post office, there since 1856, bore the name of Redwood City. The squatter-settlers, who were having to deal with Mezes for the land they occupied (and he was not known for being easy to deal with) did not thrill to the thought of renaming the place after him.

This was the only place on the Bayside that could then be called a town. At Half Moon Bay there was a village, mostly Spanish speaking, called by its citizens San Benito but by Americans Spanishtown, which may have been comparable in size to Redwood City. Purissima, four miles south, could also be called a village, as well as Pescadero, though the latter was still in Santa Cruz County. Other than these centers, the population was wholly rural and scattered.

However, the 460 farmers in the county, and their 400-odd farm laborers, according to the census of 1860, did not account for all of the population. There were some 200 general laborers, 118 shingle makers, 24 carpenters and boat makers, 20 blacksmiths and wagon makers, a dozen sailors and ship captains, a dozen butchers, and ten clerks, besides varied other occupations including hunters who bagged wild ducks for the market, cooks, and even "mantua makers", as dressmakers were sometimes called.

In the professions were five attorneys, 13 teachers, four doctors and six nurses, one dentist, one druggist, and a sole resident minister of the gospel. Scattered over the Peninsula were a dozen country stores and a dozen or fifteen saloons, most of which were also hotels. There were in 1860 four post offices: Redwood City, Woodside, Searsville, and Belmont.

Women in the Gold Rush were exceedingly rare, and even in 1860 they were still scarce. Females of all ages, from babes to grandmothers, were in San Mateo County less than a third of the population of 1860, and in the total (3,214) there were only 684 families.

This peculiar coloration of the population accounts for the tardy development of schools and churches. As schools were needed, local communities found ways to provide them. After the formation of San Mateo County (1856) such schools could get county aid by applying for it. There were no school districts as we know them until after 1860, but there were public or "common" schools in Woodside and West Union, Redwood City, Purissima, Pescadero, probably Colma, and perhaps in some other places.

In matters religious, the pattern was similar. For Catholic settlers, Dennis

Martin built a chapel on his own farm at the south end of the county, which was dedicated by Archbishop Alemany in 1856, but it did not have a resident pastor. Here, and on the Coastside, where the largest number of Spanish-speaking Catholics lived, visiting priests from the missions served the religious needs.

No Protestant pastors, it seems, were regularly stationed on the Peninsula at this time, but there are numerous contemporary references to religious services being held. A Baptist preacher lived and preached in Half Moon Bay in 1856-57, and in 1857-58, a Methodist, Rev. William Gafney, held week-day evening services in the school house at Purissima. There were services in Woodside and Redwood City but the record is sketchy; in 1860 a William Sparlock, age 23, who was living with a J. L. Snow and wife, gave his occupation as "Methodist Preacher". Pescadero must have had a congregation in the making at this time, for in 1861 a church was built.

Not until the early 1860's, roughly a decade after the wave of land buying that followed the first approval of Mexican land titles, was much serious attention given to cultural matters and community life. In 1861 the county was organized into nine school districts and from then on the number of districts, and schools, increased rapidly. Likewise in the decade of the 1860's many churches were built, and the railroad, from 1863, brought many other kinds of changes to the Peninsula.

Redwood City, viewed from the north, about 1860. The county's
first courthouse, built two years earlier, is the center building.

# V. A New County; *and the Vigilantes*

*"It is my unbiased opinion that California can and does furnish the best bad things that are obtainable in America."*   HINTON R. HELPER (1855)

It sometimes happens that a young man of good character and reputation, by indulging in some youthful indiscretion, acquires a scar that remains to plague and embarrass him as long as he lives. In a manner something like this, the young city of San Francisco awoke after a debauch of crime and corruption to find itself with a southern boundary, forming both a county line and the city limits. This invisible but doubly-legal line set a limit to the city's expansion, perhaps for all time.

This youthful indiscretion occurred in the era of the famous Vigilante Days when the city, for the second time, had so far fallen into the grip of strong criminals and weak politicians that its best people had to resort to organized violence to rescue it. The city was cleaned up but, in the process, there appeared an unexpected by-product: the birth of San Mateo County and the drawing of a boundary line that has proved to be a very troublesome thing to the City by the Golden Gate.

How corrupt can a city government get? American cities furnish many examples that are bad enough and San Francisco might not even have been the worst, though, under the conditions prevailing in California at that time, one might well expect it to be. In a city as yet without mores or customs, and with its people all busy trying to make a quick fortune, who among them would take time out to do government work unless it, too, offered a means of getting rich fast?

A type of such a government leader was an Irish immigrant, Billy Mulligan, who had taken training in New York's Tammany Hall organization. After winning popularity as a gambler and prize fighter, he found it easy to organize the city's floating population for political purposes. To begin with, he and his pals found that, through meetings euphemistically called party nominating conventions, they could sell nominations of candidates for city offices to the highest bidder—and some of the bids were really high. At one time as much as $28,000 was paid for a single nomination, with, of course, no guarantee of election.

The next step was ballot-box stuffing, which became a fine art. Voting everywhere then was carried on without any attempt at secrecy for the voter; each political party printed and circulated its own ballots and the voter simply selected, from among the ballots handed to him, the one he would turn in to the clerk at the ballot box.

So, for one of many stuffing methods, ballot boxes with false bottoms appeared, with a compartment that could be filled beforehand with the "right" ballots, and these, at a convenient moment, were shaken out and mixed with the others. Another kind had a secret device at the slot which could be fingered by the clerk as the ballots were slipped in, to shunt the "wrong" ones into a compartment where they would never be counted.

But in a short time the gangs grew bolder and did not even bother with such elaborate devices—why should they when they could control the counting of the ballots? Since no one took the trouble, or dared, to watch the process, or to protest, election returns were simply announced in the press after being made up behind closed doors to suit the boss in control.

All this had, of course, but one purpose: to plunder the public purse. San Francisco, in its first five years as an American municipality, managed to run up a debt of three and a half million dollars. But money matters were not the whole trouble. Crime ran rampant and unpunished. Burglaries and holdups were commonplace, and every few days there were murders. Few arrests were made and almost never was there a conviction.

Public indignation came to a boil as things grew worse, and the city's best people worked hard, trying to find a way to take things in hand. Their last straw was the death, on May 20, 1856, of James King of William, crusading editor of the *Bulletin,* shot down on the street in broad daylight by a Sing Sing alumnus and rival editor, James Casey. When, as usual, it became evident that the law was being used to protect the assassin instead of to punish him, a Second Vigilance Committee took over and proceeded to try Casey and other suspected criminals in its own way and to summarily hang the ones found guilty.

But this was only half of the story. This sudden resort to violence burst without warning on the city, like an unexpected outbreak of war in the midst of arbitration proceedings. By seizing control of the city, the Vigilance Committee overshadowed the fight to straighten things out by legal means. For more than a year a double-bladed plan for reform had been discussed, and had finally been enacted into a law called the Consolidation Act; in addition to new controls placed on the handling of public funds, this law provided for the consolidation of the city and county governments.

People down the Peninsula, up to then, lived in San Francisco County, and San Francisco City was their county seat. The county courthouse, sheriff, and jail were there, together with the city hall, police, and city jail. Since the county population outside the city was small, this seemed to people in the city like an expensive double system that was not necessary.

But what was more to the point, the dual government also gave an advantage to the gangsters, for often it happened that an accused criminal was brought before the county court only to be released because his attorney argued that the case belonged in the city court. The maneuver worked equally well the other way around. Furthermore, the two sets of government officials made it difficult to get up a reform movement strong enough to throw the rascals out of both city and county at the same time.

Horace Hawes, State Assemblyman for San Francisco County, who later became a resident of Redwood City, had piloted the Consolidation Bill through the lower house of the Legislature, and up to this point there was nothing in the bill about a division of the territory or the creation of a new county.

In the previous session of the Legislature (1855) some people down the Peninsula had promoted a bill for a new county to be named Raymundo. They complained that San Francisco was too far away, particularly for the people on the Coastside. Any county business they might have to attend to cost them three days of time—two in traveling there and back, and one to spend at the courthouse. Furthermore, they said, they were not properly represented in the State Legislature since the representatives elected were always from San Francisco.

The dividing line they then proposed would have been a little·more than a mile south of the present county line. This attempt was renewed in 1856, by petition, but apparently no bill was introduced, and if there was any attempt to write the plan into the Consolidation Act, Horace Hawes succeeded in preventing it in the Assembly.

But, in the Senate, the story was different, for, there, the new-county idea found some unexpected friends—some that the Peninsula did not want, and had they been consulted, would have repudiated. Who were these people? Who could want a new county so badly, and muster enough political strength to force the provision into the Consolidation Bill?

The public did not know at the time, but the answer was revealed later by Benjamin G. Lathrop, who became San Mateo County's first Clerk. In a sketch of his own life he wrote:

"In the legislature of 1856, Horace Hawes' famous consolidation act was passed, but before it could be put through Hawes had to make terms with the thieves, by adding a clause to his act cutting off about nine-tenths of the county of San Francisco, establishing what is now the county of San Mateo. Chris Lilly and Billy Mulligan, two leading chiefs of the roughs, agreed to accept that much of the county provided it could be arranged to organize a county government within one week after the passage of the act. A clause to that effect was inserted and the bill passed."

The political angle was something like this: the San Francisco "roughs" were determined to either defeat the Consolidation Bill or pull its teeth, but as the end of the legislative session drew near, they feared they could not do either. On the other hand, the reformers were adamant on certain items in the Bill but feared that in the final vote it would be defeated and all would be lost. So in the Conference Committee representing the two chambers of the legislature, a compromise was arranged.

The bitterest bone of contention was the provision that city officials must be bonded, and that a fixed ceiling be placed on the expenditures of five city departments. The roughs finally agreed to accept these but only on condition that they be given a new county, to be organized without delay.

The sequel shows that, as they planned it, this provision for immediate organization would in fact serve them up the new county on a silver platter. They would have it organized, with their own men in control, before the people down the Peninsula could know what was going on, much less have time to get up a plan of their own. They would then, at least, have something to plunder even if it couldn't be San Francisco, and they could still operate some of their rackets from behind the county line while they waited and worked for better days in the City itself.

The amendment creating the new county was written in such a hurry that several important items were overlooked: nothing was said about assuming a share of the old county's debts, and the emergency clause was omitted for some of the provisions that should have been made effective immediately. This was to cause trouble later.

The handiwork of the men who wrote it is also shown in the boundary that was drawn. Mulligan's partner in crime, Chris Lilly, was at the time owner of the Abbey House on the hill, at the intersection of Mission Street and San Jose Avenue in the present Daly City. This place, if it could be within the new county, would be a very convenient center, just outside the city, for operations of the gang. So instead of placing the line as proposed the previous year, a mile south of the Abbey House, it was made to run through "a point in the county road one fourth of a mile north-easterly from the house kept and occupied by C. E. Lilly."

The law as a whole took effect on July 1, as bills normally do, but the election to organize the new county was ordered to be held on May 12. Three men were named in the law itself to supervise the election: Dr. R. O. Tripp of Woodside, John Johnston of Half Moon Bay, and Charles Clark of Colma. But Tripp refused to take any part in the affair, so the other two proceeded without him, setting up thirteen precincts, and calling the election on the given day.

But what an election it turned out to be! Johnston and Clark were surprised to find they had very little to do with it. The gang had its slate of candidates for office, of course, among whom were Billy Mulligan's brother, Bernard, for sheriff, and Chris Lilly's bartender, Robert Gray, for county clerk. They made no pretense of campaigning for their candidates; the obvious idea of the early election was to prevent anyone's campaigning. They simply took possession of the polls in three of the thirteen princincts and planned "returns" from those three that would elect their key men in spite of anything that might be done in the other ten.

The three selected precincts were the Colma region, where the polling place was in Lilly's saloon; the Laguna area, which comprised the valley now filled with the Crystal Springs Lakes, where the population consisted of scattered farmers who would make no trouble; and Belmont, where the population was also small and scattered, and where lived a partner in the deal, Ex-Governor of California, John McDougal. He had been persuaded to support the gangsters' plan on condition that Belmont be made the county seat.

One of the first to discover the machine in operation on election day was W. D. Harrington, a farmer who had lived in the Laguna valley some five years. He later testifed in court that upon arrival at the polling place about eight o'clock in the morning he found a group of complete strangers in charge. "I asked who they were", he said under oath, "and was told that Mr. Pat Hickey had been there with a party,

A Sunday school class of the 1880's (Menlo Park Episcopal Church).
Most of the pioneer churches and schools, shown in this section,
are flourishing today in modern buildings.

First church in San Mateo, St. Matthew's Catholic (1864). (Below)
St. Denis Chapel, built by Dennis Martin on his farm near Searsville (1853). From a painting.

St. Matthew's Episcopal Church, San Mateo (1865).

Congregational Church, San Mateo (1868).

Elementary school on Broadway, Redwood City.

San Mateo County Teachers Institute, 1885-1886. (Inset) John Greer of Woodside, donor of land for the county's first schoolhouse.

(Above) La Honda Elementary School.
(Below) Tunis District School, still open, 1963.

and organized, and voted, and gone; - - - I asked if they were ready to receive votes; they said yes; I replied that they had not a full board; they had only four, and the law required five; they pointed to one who was asleep, snoring melodiously; he then got up—he was pock-marked and seemed to be sick; I suggested that they should let some man come in his place who could attend to his duties; this they refused; wished to inquire who they were before voting; could not learn; a Mr. Moss who was with me knew the pock-marked man as 'Liverpool Jack'; I have seen three of the others since but do not know their names; 'Liverpool Jack' lives in San Francisco; none of them live in the precinct; they kept the poll all day; I left at 2 or 3 o'clock; during my stay there were about 43 votes, legal and illegal, put in the box; there were not over 25 adult males in the precinct; - - - ."

The official returns for this precinct, when made up after election day, showed that 297 votes had been cast. The voters' names were all on the tally list. Where did they come from? Someone later discovered the strange ones on the passenger list of a steamer recently arrived in port at San Francisco.

The Colma precinct was similarly made to show some 500 votes cast where there were not more than 50 or 60 eligible voters. Here Edward Hancock, a hotel man of Redwood City, testified to being present at the Abbey House on the day after the election when the votes were being counted. " - - - When they took up a ballot", he said, "they would call out ten for so and so; six or seven for another, and so on - - - ; one time they took a ballot, they called out two for Ackerson, but someone said, 'there's no use, transfer them to Mulligan, Ackerson has resigned'; did not appear to be at all governed by the number of ballots in the box, always called out more - - -."

At Belmont the polling place was in McDougal's home and one of the election judges was Benjamin Fenwick, a gang candidate for county supervisor. There apparently were no outside witnesses to the counting of the ballots at the Belmont polls. The final hurdle for the gang was the summing up for the whole county, which, by law, must be made under the direction of Clark and Johnston. These two men made an attempt to study the reports behind closed doors at the American House in Redwood City, but a little gun play brought them into line and they meekly agreed not to make any fuss about the obviously doctored returns.

The result of the election was not a clean sweep for the interlopers, but their key men were in, with a total vote cast of more than 1,800. The county's whole population was not more than 2,500 and in those days women did not vote.

But, it was just at this point that the men who were so brazenly planning to take over the government of the Peninsula were frightened by an attack in their rear. Just three days after this absurd election, James King of William was shot. Within a week he was dead and the Vigilance Committee was going into action. Neither the shooting of King nor the rise of the Vigilance Committee had anything directly to do with the Consolidation Act or this election, but the Committee's action had the effect of changing the entire scene.

In a matter of days after King's death his murderer was hanged, together with another criminal; in time there were more hangings, and other undesirables, including Mulligan and Lilly, were required to take ship for other parts of the world. On

Sunday, May 25, the newspaper *Wide West* described conditions in San Francisco as follows:

"There is an astonishing dearth of general news in the city. No courts are in session, and no rows are in progress; no street fights, or bar-room difficulties to report. A drunken man in the street even is now rarely seen, San Francisco was never so quiet, so orderly as she is now, under what some of the papers denominate the 'reign of terror'."

And the same paper, in deep mourning for King, carried the following editorial titled "The San Mateo Outrage":

"The actors in the late frauds at San Mateo must not go unpunished. Still less must those who have been elevated to position and power by the disgraceful incidents of that election be permitted to keep the rewards of their audacity and crime. Here is a field for law to vindicate itself in prompt and efficient action. Let not the opportunity pass unimproved. For if we would have order, we must have justice as a consequence of legal action. We do not wish soon to see another week like the past. We do not wish again to see the people compelled to do this work for which they pay officials. But better months of such action than submission to wrong. And we warn those whose duty it is to proceed in this matter to act, unless they wish to lose all future opportunity for action."

Pursuant to this warning, and in the new atmosphere of enforced order and calm, suit was brought to nullify the results of San Mateo County's corrupt election. Fortunately, the county judge, an honest man, chosen through an oversight by the gang, was one of the Peninsula's best citizens, Benjamin I. Fox. His court, sitting at Belmont in the Angelo House, heard the evidence. No one even appeared for the defendants, for their leaders were now in exile, and the returns from the three corrupted precincts were declared null and void. As a result, the returns from the other ten precincts elected the county's officials, and the county seat went to Redwood City instead of Belmont.

There was one absurd sequel, an anti-climax, or perhaps a fitting catharsis to the whole affair. John McDougal brought suit to contest the election of John Johnston as county supervisor. The decision was not rendered until October, 1856, after the Vigilance Committee had retired and things had settled down to quiet routine, and it brought a surprise for everyone.

The hastily written paragraph in the Consolidation Act, ordering the election to be held on May 12, did not contain an emergency clause giving it immediate force of law. Hence it did not become law, said the court, until July 1, and the election held before that day was completely illegal and without effect.

So the county had no government! Yet by the time the decision was announced, officials had been functioning as a government for some time and actions had been taken that could not be undone. It was decided therefore to proceed regularly for the time being and try to get things legalized by the next legislature. This was done in due course, and a new bona fide election was held during 1857, removing the stigma of illegitimacy from San Mateo County.

Perhaps the most fitting conclusion to this part of the story is to be found in the report of San Mateo's first grand jury, dated August 11, 1856, which contained this comment: "Had not the prompt and decided action of the people of San Francisco relieved us of the presence of the most desperate of this gang, the consequences to the people of this county would have been disastrous in the extreme."

The Legislature of 1857, at the same time that it cleared away the legal cloud hanging over the county's government, settled some interesting questions about boundaries. On the north, the boundary line set up by the Consolidation Act was a succession of lines from landmark to landmark. Instead of this haphazard deline- ation, the new law set up a straight line that coincided with a section line of the United States land survey, yet left the boundary essentially where it had been.

On the south, the matter was a little more complex. The line drawn when the counties were created (1851) ran from the mouth of San Francisquito Creek "up the middle of said creek to its source in the Santa Cruz Mountains; thence due west to the ocean and three miles therein". This was plain enough until it came to locating the source of San Francisquito Creek. This creek was formed by at least two tributaries, either of which could easily be taken as the main stream, and the difference between the two sources involved a large section of Coastside territory, roughly that lying between San Gregorio and Tunitas creeks.

This dispute over the boundary between San Francisco and Santa Cruz counties had dragged on for six years without definite settlement, but with Santa Cruz county in actual possession of at least the major part of the disputed territory. Now the new law, piloted through the Legislature by Timothy Guy Phelps, neatly put the whole block of disputed land inside San Mateo County by simply changing the description to read, "up the middle of said creek (San Francisquito), following the middle of the *south branch* thereof to its source in the Santa Cruz Mountains" etc. as before. This brought the boundary out to the coast at San Gregorio.

The Pescadero area was growing, meanwhile, in population but the people there were discontented with their situation in Santa Cruz County because of the barrier of the chalk mountain slope between them and their county seat. Encouraged by the boundary of San Mateo County being brought nearer to them, they began a campaign to get their territory annexed to San Mateo County. Their plea was that they were "forty miles north of the county seat of Santa Cruz County, with an impassable road most of the year—and never can there be a good road to the Santa Cruz County Seat".

After several attempts to get action, it came finally in the Legislature of 1868—the area north of the chalk mountain was transferred, and became a part of San Mateo County, with several square miles of Bútano forest area thrown in for good measure.

Quarrels over the seat of government have been common to all U. S. county histories, and San Mateo's is no exception to the rule.

First, when the county was barely five years old, some ambitious owners of real estate, in what later became the Homestead Tract of San Mateo, had enough political friends to get an act through the Legislature authorizing an election on the question of moving the county seat from Redwood City to some new place, just where not being specified.

This apparently came as a bolt from the blue to the people of Redwood City, for it took some investigating to find out who was at the bottom of it. San Mateo was not yet a town that could figure as a rival for the courthouse, but the promoters called their place San Mateo Villa, and planned a courthouse out in the country, as things were then, approximately at the present Barneson Avenue. The election was held but Redwood City won by a comfortable margin and the worry seemed over.

But the real fight came later. After the building of the railroad, San Mateo grew rapidly and developed some strong arguments why the courthouse should be there instead of at Redwood City: it had the same name as the county, hence moving to San Mateo would avoid confusion; furthermore, San Mateo was more centrally located and more accessible, particularly to the people of the Coastside.

When an earthquake wrecked the courthouse (1868), the time seemed right for action, and Alvinza Hayward made the first move by deeding to the county certain lots in his San Mateo subdivision—on condition that the courthouse be erected there.

In the election which followed, one that was ordered by the County Supervisors, Redwood City won again but this time by the dangerously narrow margin of only ten votes in 1,396. Encouraged by this near-win, San Mateo, alleging irregularities in the voting, persuaded the Supervisors to order a new election a bare six months after the first one.

This time, the campaign was bitterly fought and there were probably more irregularities than ever. The whole county lined up geographically, the south favoring Redwood City, the north and Coastside for San Mateo. Fearing defeat at the polls, the southerners took the matter to court. Faxon D. Atherton brought suit, denying any illegalities in the first election, and seeking a court order to forbid the holding of another.

In this situation, the time of the election was approaching, and what with appeals and counter-appeals to the State Supreme Court, no quick decision was in sight. So the attorneys in the case entered into an agreement, stipulating that the election would be held but that the results would not be considered legal until the court had rendered its decision. The whole matter then was brought to an end in a dramatic anti-climax. San Mateo won the election by a large majority, but after eight months of suspense, the court granted a writ prohibiting its being held!

Since then the question has never been seriously raised, though threats have been made from time to time, and plans have been proposed for a county civic center somewhere in open country, but the age of easy travel by automobile has now made the matter of location relatively unimportant.

Linden Towers, dream-house of James C. Flood, Menlo Park.

# VI. Many Mansions: *the men who built them*

*"It had been the dream of ancient alchemists to transmute base metals into gold. The Californians of '49 had a harder task. They had to transmute gold into human values."*                                    BLAKE ROSS

The "beautiful gothic residence" that Bayard Taylor saw at San Mateo, if it had remained in Boston, would have been just a good house, but in California of the 1850's it was something to see; when first built there was nothing in the Peninsula countryside to equal it.

Yet nobody would call it grand or spectacular. An all-around glassed-in porch gave it rather a feeling of relaxation, and of oneness with the flat earth on which it stood. The windows of its upper story, on the other hand, looked out from sharply pointed gables that carried the eye upward—up to the peak where roof ornaments pointing to the sky gave still more added height; and for a touch of Victorian elegance, a frieze of pendants hung like dripping icicles from the eaves. It sat modestly, well back from the road, surrounded by a vast expanse of lawns with ancient oak trees and winding driveways.

The house had the further distinction of having been freighted bodily by ship from New England, and the romantic fame of being the home of the rich and popular William D. M. Howard, San Francisco merchant, and his sixteen-year-old bride.

The bride had dropped as if from heaven into the arms of widower Howard. Her father, Dr. Joseph Henry Poett, was en route with his family from Chile to England and had taken a ship that was to visit San Francisco before going around the Horn. Happening to arrive at the Embarcadero when the Gold Rush was at fever pitch, like all ships at that time and place, it was abandoned in the harbor as all hands rushed off to the gold fields.

Young Agnes Poett—so the family story goes—as she stepped ashore on the dockless beach, was helped by a gallant and handsome man whose attention she seems to have distracted from his business of scouting for merchandise that ships might happen to bring. For her part, she confided later to her children, it was a case of love at first sight, and in this respect Mr. Howard could not have been far behind, for it all happened in the year 1849, and on July 9 they were married.

Howard was apparently grateful for his bride, who came so unexpectedly into

El Cerrito, San Mateo's first pre-fabricated dwelling.

William D. M. Howard, wealthy, esteemed San Francisco merchant, shipped over twenty pre-fabricated dwellings from Boston in the 1850's to meet a housing shortage. He set up one of the homes in San Mateo (1850) for his sixteen-year-old bride, Agnes Poett.

California's womanless world, for he was very generous with his wife's family. His firm, Mellus & Howard, had acquired Rancho San Mateo (6,438 acres) from the grantee, Cayetano Arenas, and he now retired from the firm, took over the rancho and planned to live on it as his country estate. But large portions of it were deeded or willed to Dr. Poett and other members of his family.

In this way the Howard-Poett clan planted their family tree on the former Rancho San Mateo, and set the pattern for genteel living down the Peninsula. William D. M. Howard himself died prematurely in 1856 but his very young widow, Agnes, married his brother George and, in due course, various members of the family became participating members in the community. Alfred Poett was a civil engineer; George Howard Jr. became an architect; and various other relatives entered business or the professions. Julia Howard Beylard became known for her gift of a parish house to St. Matthew's Episcopal Church. Already the family had given land for St. Matthew's and for the San Mateo Congregational Church.

The original Howard mansion, named *El Cerrito* after the nearby small hill since known as The Mound, enjoyed a long history. Its original site would now be on De Sabla Road. The building itself was finally moved to Roehampton Road where it became, in 1910, the Hillsborough Town Hall. It has since been demolished.

The Howard-Poett family were a full decade ahead of any other well-to-do settlers like them, but in 1860 they could see that a change was coming. In that year D. O. Mills, conservative millionaire banker and financier, and his brother-in-law Ansel I. Easton, who recorded his occupation as "gentleman", each bought 1,500 acres of Buri Buri land, now in Millbrae and Burlingame. In the same year, John Parrott, another banker with a large fortune, bought the Fred Macondray place of some 500 acres, now embracing the Baywood tract in San Mateo.

Farther south, in the same year, Faxon D. Atherton, a New Englander who had married in Chile and accumulated both a family and a fortune there, bought 500 acres, now in the city that bears his name. He was shortly followed by Thomas H. Selby, wealthy industrialist and Mayor of San Francisco, who bought up a tract of equal extent bordering Atherton's on the north.

Why, suddenly, all this land buying? The San Francisco and San José Railroad Company had just been organized. Railroad talk was nothing new but now, it appeared, things were going to be done. Investors were moving to take advantage of the rising land values, but their purchases foreshadowed something more than this. Theirs were the first steps in the establishment of many elaborate country residences which the railroad would bring within easy reach of offices and social engagements in the city.

The era of Peninsula estates, begun thus in the 'Sixties, boomed in the 'Seventies and 'Eighties, and even extended well into the Twentieth Century. Wealthy men's mansions—some modest, others bizarre and flamboyant—would be for more than half a century the dominant feature of the Peninsula scene.

The railroad was the springboard of this development. An early attempt to build a line, under the ambitious name of the Pacific and Atlantic Railroad, had died in the depression of 1855. Despite the new company's more modest name, The San

Francisco and San José Railroad, the hope was still generally cherished that any rails leading out of San Francisco would tie in somewhere with a transcontinental line. On the new company's opening day 585 shares were subscribed at $100 each, with $5,750 cash paid in. By October 24, 1860, a contract was signed for the actual building of the road.

But before dirt could begin to fly or rails could be ordered from the East, more money had to be in sight. To supplement private capital, the City and County of San Francisco voted to bond itself for $300,000 worth of railroad stock. San Mateo County took $100,000 worth, and Santa Clara County $200,000. To help the campaign for this popular vote, a ground-breaking ceremony was held May 1, 1861, at San Francisquito Creek. The bonds carried on May 21, and by November of that year the grade was completed from Belmont to Santa Clara. All this grading was done with pick-and-shovel and horse cart.

The laying of track was delayed by the Civil War; fear of British intervention held up shipment by sea of rails and locomotives; and war-time inflation kept driving prices up. Also, the winter of 1861-62 was a very wet one; but while it caused much damage to the grading, it also taught the engineers some useful lessons about drainage.

The company's engineers wanted the road to go into San Francisco by the most direct route, along the Bay shore, but for several reasons it was decided instead to go through Colma, to the west of the San Bruno Mountains. There was more population that way, which would mean more local business in passengers and freight, as well as more popular support for the enterprise; and it would be cheaper to build because the bay-shore route called for a long bridge past Visitacion Valley, approximately the route of the present Bayshore Freeway. On the other route the only serious engineering hurdle was the Bernal Cut.

By summer of 1863, rails were arriving and track was being laid. We can well understand the excitement when the first locomotive chugged its way into Redwood City on this almost-first railroad on the Pacific Coast. It was preceded only by a kind of steam-powered street car that ran from downtown San Francisco out through the sand hills to the Mission, a similar one in Oakland, and a line from Sacramento to Folsom.

Also, this was a local enterprise –conceived and built by local capitalists and local engineers, and largely by popular effort. Property values were already going up in a wild spiral: one man in San Mateo reported being offered $1,000 for land that formerly was hardly worth $50.

When track was laid as far as Mayfield (South Palo Alto), the Peninsula could not wait any longer—there had to be a big celebration. On October 17, 1863, a special train was run, carrying all the prominent citizens and company officials, and as many more as could get on, from San Francisco to the end of the line, then back for a picnic lunch on the banks of San Francisquito Creek. Food and liquid spirits were there in abundance, and a rousing time was had by all. The next day, Sunday, October 18, regular passenger service was inaugurated with one train daily down and back.

By January 16, 1864, the line was completed to San Jose; it then became that city's turn to stage a giant celebration and, from February 18, two trains daily were put in service, leaving San Francisco at 8:00 A. M. and 4:00 P. M., and leaving San Jose at 7:30 A. M. and 3:30 P. M. The scheduled time for each run was two hours and twenty minutes. Stops en route were at Bernal, San Miguel, School House (Colma), Twelve Mile House, San Bruno, Seventeen Mile House (Millbrae), San Mateo, Belmont, Redwood City, Menlo Park, Mayfield, Mountain View, Lawrence's, Santa Clara, San Jose. The first San Francisco station was at Fourth and Brannan streets; later, for a period of years, it was at Market and Valencia.

On June 4, 1864, when the contractor officially turned over the road to its owners, a special train was run for inspection purposes. On the return trip it went all out for a speed record. This "lightning train", its puffing little engine blowing smoke and cinders from a funnel-shaped stack almost as large as the boiler, made the fifty miles from San José to San Francisco in one hour and fifteen minutes. But, the news reporter complained, three minutes should be allowed for being detained in San Mateo, and at least as many more for time lost driving cattle off the track. Anyway, he didn't ever want to travel any faster!

It is safe to assume that everybody on the Peninsula who had a little money to spare bought some railroad stock, and some prominent Peninsulans were on the company's Board of Directors: C. B. Polhemus, who surveyed and promoted the town of San Mateo, and Peter Donahue, who lived for a time in San Mateo and was the founder of San Francisco's Union Iron Works, which built the locomotive named California. Another was H. M. Newhall, founder of a still-prominent California family.

A few years later, under the new name of the Southern Pacific Company, with Timothy Guy Phelps as President, building on to the south from San José was begun, but the railway was still a local company. That it soon should pass into the hands of the "Big Four" to become a part of a state-wide railroad monopoly, was not the desire or intent of these men of San Mateo County.

The building of the railroad was followed almost immediately by a succession of men with famous names moving to establish homes down the Peninsula. They were usually called summer places at first but they later became permanent residences. The man who led off, ironically, was William C. Ralston, who, though he actually was as dependent on the railroad as anyone, took delight in embarrassing it by beating its trains with his horses.

In 1864, simultaneously with his founding of the Bank of California, Ralston bought Count Leonetto Cipriani's place in Belmont and enlarged it to serve as his summer home, and for elaborate entertainment. It has been said that he added only wings and ells, but the reverse of this statement would be nearer the truth. In the making of Ralston's mansion, Cipriani's house became only a small wing, and what Ralston added was a house with more wings.

The Sisters of Notre Dame, who currently own the property, have identified Cipriani's portion, as distinguished from Ralston's construction, by the style of its interior trim, and by an elegant fireplace of white marble, different in design from any in Ralston's building. When completed, Cipriani's portion constituted the east-

The "San Mateo" coupled to a train of the 1860's.

Menlo Park was one of the earliest stations on the San Francisco-
San José Railroad. Early commuters included Stanford, Hopkins,
and Flood.

Primitive train crossing San Francisquito Creek by the Palo Alto.
One of the ancient, twin trees stands today.

San Carlos Station was built in 1888 when Stanford University was
constructed. Notice the same type of quarried stone in the walls.

The engine, "California", was built by San Francisco's Union Iron
Works for the San Francisco-San José Railroad.

The daily stage leaves for Half Moon Bay and Pescadero after meeting the train at San Mateo.

ward wing of the house, parallelling Ralston's ballroom. A later owner, Dr. A. M. Gardner, extended Cipriani's wing and topped it with a third story.

A Ralston contribution were the parquet floors of walnut, maple, and mahogany, laid in all the central rooms, and without thresholds under his wide, rising doors, so as to permit the use of the whole as one great hall for dancing. His also were the silver-plated door knobs, the French-imported cut glass doors, and the central foyer with opera-box balconies. Besides his grand banquet hall, there was a ballroom with plate glass mirrors in imitation of the famous Hall of Mirrors in Versailles. Outside were croquet grounds and a bowling alley, plus a gymnasium equipped for Turkish baths.

Ralston's great social events were as spectacular as he knew how to make them, and spectacular things were his forte. He was one of those rare persons who was able to live a life of personal showmanship without seeming to offend good taste. If there ever was a tendency to shudder at his glamorous affairs, the warmth and sincerity of his personality dissipated it, plus the fact that it was all for a purpose: to enhance the greatness of his City of San Francisco.

He loved to spring surprises, such as on the occasion when his dinner guests waited in growing suspense with no dinner in sight and the hour growing late, until finally a large door began slowly to rise with apparently no hands touching it, revealing a long banquet table with a pig-tailed Chinaman standing behind each chair. The serving of the many-course meal lasted until about midnight.

Guests for these occasions were sometimes put up for the night in his fifty bedrooms provided for just this purpose, and often they were brought down from San Francisco by special train and returned in the same way. On one occasion, at least, he telegraphed his wife during the day to prepare for fifty guests for dinner that night.

Ralston got a great thrill out of driving with his four-horse carry-all or *char-a-bancs* to San Francisco and back, beating the train. He managed it by driving at breakneck speed between relay stations, where fresh horses were harnessed and ready, at intervals along the way; with a few quick motions, they were exchanged for his panting and sweating steeds, the reins were handed to him, and the fresh horses, knowing his touch, were off with a leap in a new cloud of dust.

His route, in certain seasons, was through Colma and, in others, via the new San Bruno Toll Road—over the present San Mateo Avenue in San Bruno and into San Francisco along the Bay shore. His relay stations on this route seem to have been at San Mateo, Cunningham's San Bruno House at the railroad crossing on San Mateo Avenue, at Sierra Point, and at the Toll House in Visitacion Valley.

The grand climax of a day well spent, was to arrive in Belmont, with wind-blown guests, cross the track just ahead of the train, and reach his house just after dark. This way his mansion came impressively into view all ablaze with light from his own gas plant (which his neighbors could use too if they wished); his gate swung open of its own accord as his carriage approached, and he braked to a dramatic stop under the massive *porte cochere* where everybody climbed down.

Ralston died in 1875 while taking his customary swim in the Bay at North Beach—a variant relaxation from driving to Belmont—and as the tragedy coincided with the closing of his bank in the midst of a run on its cash, his enemies insisted that he had committed suicide. But no water was found in his lungs, and his life insurance was paid promptly. The immediate cause of death, as the autopsy surgeon put it, was "asphyxia with cerebral congestion", caused, presumably, by anxiety, the hot day, and over-exercise in the cold water.

William Sharon took over his property and lived in the Belmont home. After this it became a girls' seminary, then a mental hospital, and, since 1922, it has been a part of the College of Notre Dame.

Meanwhile, San Mateo too was acquiring famous names. In fact, with its first consciousness as a village, San Mateo awoke to find itself encircled by the acreages of prominent men.

Hitherto it had been a mere stopping place on the highway; now it became an adjunct to the railroad. The first town plat, drawn in 1862, was five blocks square with the railway station at the center. With no more stagecoach traffic along the highway, the San Mateo House now became a residence for Captain Edward Taylor, and a new hotel was built near the station. Also, Henry Husing now moved his roadside country store into town at the corner of Third Avenue and B Street.

The rapid growth of a completely new town was important enough in the making of history, but the encircling process more especially caught the limelight. There were the Howard lands to the north and west; the Macondray place, now Baywood, was owned by the famous banker John Parrott; and the village soon learned that all the outlying land to the south and east of it had been bought by a stranger from Amador County named Alvinza Hayward. The story whispered about was that this newcomer, who had struck it rich in mining, had started out as a prospector on money that his wife earned by taking in washing.

However little truth there may have been in this rumor, it is a fact that Hayward worked as an ox-driver or bull-whacker, dragging logs to a sawmill, while he struggled to develop a mine which he felt sure held the possibility of making him rich. He bought timber for his mine from his employer and borrowed his oxen on the weekend to haul it there.

Years afterward, when his one-time employer was dead and he himself was rich beyond even his early dreams, he paid a visit to the haunts of his struggles with poverty and was shocked to recall that he never had paid for the load of timber. He found, in fact, that the account still stood against him in the neatly-kept ledger— $261.50. When the widow refused a check for nearly double the amount, insisting that she wanted only the payment of the original debt, he persuaded her to have her son figure the interest for the elapsed time at one percent a month, compounded every six months. This took considerable time and everybody in the neighborhood had a part in it, each one coming up with a different answer. But when agreement was finally reached and the report sent to Mr. Hayward, he sent his check for the total amount: $2,100.

Hayward's mine did justify his faith in it and was finally sold for a neat sum, said to have been eight million dollars. He, at first, built a modest home on his San

James Clair Flood

Leland Stanford

William Chapman Ralston

Darius Ogden Mills

John Parrott

Faxon Dean Atherton

Thomas Henry Selby

Antoine Borel

William C. Ralston's "Belmont" as he built it. The right front wing, which was orginally the Cipriani home, has since been extended and topped with another story.

Hayward Park, home of Alvinza Hayward.

The wing in the right background (above) was added for hotel purposes after Hayward's death. The entire structure was destroyed by fire in 1920. During Hayward's time, the estate included a race track, fenced-in deer and elk, and a lake with ducks and swans.

Mateo property, then opened an office in San Francisco and proceeded to acquire more millions by dealing in mining stocks.

To the people of San Mateo, he seemed forbidding and aloof, yet he made himself a part of the community by building the town's first water works, opening a new subdivision that provided space for it to grow, and by starting one of the popular but unsuccessful attempts to get the county seat moved from Redwood City to San Mateo. Also, he customarily responded to community appeals for various needs and charities, though sometimes under protest, just to discourage any overdoing of this sort of thing.

Apparently, he did not want to be aloof from ordinary folk. He had been a small-town citizen before—a practicing attorney in Canton, upper New York state—and he liked this way of life; his stablemen and gardeners reported that with them even his profanity was of the usual ox-driver's type. On the other hand, he could greatly impress callers at his office in San Francisco with his refinement and gentlemanly manners—which were quite in keeping with reports about his British ancestors, one of whom is said to have been Lord Mayor of London.

In the 1880's the stock market having been kind to him, he began the building of a more pretentious mansion. Others had done it, D. O. Mills to the north, and James Flood to the south, besides many lesser ones between, so why not he?

His mansion turned out to be a massive, three-storied structure, with a square tower that narrowed to a point two stories higher. It seemed to be all windows—an endless number of them, all rectangular in shape; and the roof was a profusion of gables of all sizes and pointing in all directions. Rectangles and triangles everywhere gave it a severity of design that seemed to fit the owner's somber appearance, and it went along strangely with the fact that in this massive structure lived only the master, his wife and one daughter. Even social events to brighten it up seem to have been few, or non-existent.

But the mansion and its outbuildings were surrounded by beautiful lawns and ornamental trees, and to the south of it, in the section of San Mateo between the railroad and El Camino Real, now known as Hayward Park, was Hayward's park. A racetrack formed its limits, and in the enclosure was a tightly fenced park with deer, elk, a pond with ducks and swans, beautifully landscaped orchards and ornamental trees. The stables too were fabulous—stalls furnished like the interior of a house, silver mounted harness, and fine carriages.

Hayward seemingly made the transition from prospector to gentleman rather easily, but once having done this he did not otherwise change. He is said to have worn to his dying day (1904) the costume of the early California business man— Prince Albert coat and tall silk hat. The only variation he indulged in was when he made a trip to the mines; then it was still the Prince Albert coat but instead of the stove-pipe hat, he wore a wide-brimmed, black slouch hat, and high boots.

At home, in his ebony costume, he was driven every morning to the station—in a black carriage with black horses—and was solemnly met in the same way at night. His home, after his death, with large wings added, became the fashionable Peninsula Hotel. But in 1920 it was consumed in a spectacular fire. The former entrance to his estate from El Camino Real is now Hayward Avenue, and some of the trees that once adorned his yard are still growing in parkways along Hayward, Palm, and Laurel avenues.

It was characteristic of John Parrott that, unlike the later bonanza kings, he was known in San Francisco not so much for a palatial home as for having built the city's first fireproof business block (1852), and for having done it solidly and economically out of cut granite imported from China, and with imported Chinese labor. A man with the Midas touch for making money, by the time he got around to building a home down the Peninsula, being rich was no novelty. Already past middle life, he was not interested in displaying his wealth; he wanted a summer home for his wife and seven young children.

With typical foresight, Parrott had bought the land in 1860. Some eight years later, when he built his house approximately on the site of the present Baywood Apartments on West Third Avenue, it was large and comfortable but not showy, nor was it distinguished in any particular way by its architecture. Later on, it became the permanent family home, not just for summers, and John spent much of his time there until his death in 1883.

As his daughters grew up and married, three of them built houses similar to the family home and lived in San Mateo: Mary (Mrs. Christian de Guigne) on the site of the present Banjamin Franklin Hotel, Abby Josephine (Mrs. A. H. Payson) beside it in the Fourth Avenue area. Her husband, Captain Payson, became San Mateo's first mayor when the town was incorporated in 1894. Grace (Mrs. Robert Y. Hayne) lived on West Fifth Avenue (the south side) where, only recently, her house was demolished.

The son, John Parrott Jr., married Mary E. Donohoe and lived in the family mansion. The Donohoe and Parrott families were doubly united, for Christine, the youngest Parrott girl, was married to Joseph A. Donohoe, brother of Mary, and lived near Menlo Park, now in Atherton. The Parrott family were the donors of the land for St. Matthew's Catholic Church.

The homes of Parrott's daughters formed part of an inner circle of smaller estates that sealed off the village of San Mateo from direct contact with the County Road (El Camino Real). Beginning at the north was Captain Edward Taylor's home, formerly the San Mateo Hotel, standing in a ten-acre yard filled with oaks and laurels. The house, now on the corner of Second Avenue and El Camino Real, forms part of the nurses' quarters for Mills Memorial Hospital. Then came the de Guignes and the Paysons.

In the present Central Park was another landmark. C. B. Polhemus first lived here, then Peter Donahue, and its final owner was Captain William H. Kohl, who was engaged in the Alaska fur trade. It was Kohl who in 1874 built the ornamental stone-and-iron fence that still beautifully shields the park from the highway traffic.

To the north, besides the various members of the Howard-Poett family, but on a portion of their Rancho San Mateo, lived Henri Barroilhet, a French banker of San Francisco. His land later became the home of Mrs. Jennie Henderson, sister of

Templeton Crocker. Adjoining him on the east, but west of the San Mateo Park subdivision, was the vineyard and winery of Gustave Mahe, President of the French Savings and Loan Society of San Francisco. Another portion of this same rancho was sold in 1866 to Anson Burlingame, but the only immediate effect of this sale was to put the name of Burlingame on the map for future reference.

North of the grant line lay the lands of Buri Buri, of which two large portions were purchased in 1860 by Ansel I. Easton and D. O. Mills. Easton's 1,500 acres extended from Burlingame's Sanchez Avenue to the creek at Adeline Drive, named after his wife, Adeline Mills, and from the Bay to the valley of the lakes on the west. The Eastons were married in San Francisco in 1857, and had by 1860 returned from a honeymoon trip in which they were shipwrecked off the stormy coast of Cape Hatteras. The bride was taken off in a lifeboat under the rule of women and children first, while the groom stayed to go down with the ship but was miraculously thrown clear and rescued.

The California scene gave their romance another interesting turn: they wanted to live in a genuine adobe house, and Ansel let nothing stand in the way of their doing so. "Chino" Sánchez, former owner of this portion of Rancho Buri Buri, had built an adobe house near Sánchez Avenue, and Easton had this building torn apart in order to use the adobe bricks. Blissfully unmindful of earthquakes, he built his lower story of heavy timbers and topped it with adobe walls for the upper story. The cost of the operation was his own little secret, about which he seemed rather sensitive, for he never shared it with anyone.

This house stood on what later became the Charles S. Howard place, west of the intersection of Easton Drive with Vancouver Avenue, Today's Easton Drive, bordered by eucalyptus trees, was the entrance road. Two generations of Eastons lived here, though the house itself was not so permanent. After the stern warning given by the earthquake of 1868, it was replaced by a more dependable structure, but this in turn, was demolished after being damaged by a falling tree, and a third house took its place.

Darius Ogden Mills, consistent with his reputation as a safe and conservative financier, bought his 1,500 acres adjoining Easton's in 1860, but did no more with it until the railroad was actually in operation and his title to the land was cleared beyond a shadow of doubt. His original cost was recorded as $10,000 but to protect this investment he was obliged to buy up another claim because José de la Cruz Sánchez had signed more than one mortgage. After this, he joined with Easton and James Lux in a suit to quiet title to all Buri Buri lands, which may have run the total cost of his portion as high as twenty dollars an acre.

When all this was finished and done, but not until then, Mr. Mills began the construction of his mansion—a three-story frame building, large and stately. It had two full stories for living, besides an all-purpose basement containing the kitchen, and a third story for servants' quarters behind a mansard roof. On one side was a large porch overlooking a sweep of land toward the County Road and the Bay, and on the opposite side was a massive *porte cochere* covering the main entrance.

The first floor contained a spacious, high-ceilinged living room, dining room, music room, library, and billiard room, and a grand staircase leading to an art gallery and stately bedrooms above. Two of the bedrooms, finished respectively in mother-of-pearl and ebony, were for the master and lady of the house. Another became known as the Grant Room after General Grant, Ex-President of the United States, slept there as a guest of the Mills family.

Mills called his place Millbrae—a combination of his name with a Scottish word meaning a rolling meadowland, for this is precisely what his acreage was. Part of it he used as pasturage for his Millbrae Dairy, which turned out to be about the most durable dairy on the Peninsula—the last to be crowded out by urban development. Another portion he planted to eucalyptus trees which quickly grew into a small forest. For water supply, he built dams in the upper ravines, creating small reservoirs that were soon hidden by trees.

But his special delight were his large, glass-covered greenhouse and his collection of exotic shrubs which he personally gathered from all parts of the world. These shrubs and rare trees he planted in a landscaped stretch of lawn around his mansion. All were botanical rarities and some were plants of indescribable beauty.

Long after Mr. Mills' death the mansion was kept intact, although the now-famous family, even before this date, preferred to live in New York. The daughter, Elizabeth, had become the wife of Whitelaw Reid, publisher of the New York *Tribune,* and President McKinley's Ambassador to Great Britain. In later years the grandson, Ogden L. Mills, became President Hoover's Secretary of the Treasury. For some years, the family made trips by special train for a vacation at Millbrae, bringing along horses, automobiles, and an army of servants. Later this expeditionary corps fell off to an annual visit by a family representative to look after financial affairs. But still the structure was unchanged except that, during World War II, it was used as a seamen's rest home.

Finally the house, damaged by termites and general deterioration, became an expensive liability and had to be demolished (it burned in the process), but the landscaped area around it was potentially a beautiful park, and maps published in local newspapers showed this to be the plan. But unfortunately this was not done. Instead, the whole rolling hill, including the rare shrubs, was ruthlessly bulldozed out and leveled for apartments and a shopping center. The mansion and grounds occupied approximately today's block of apartments west of Ogden Drive, and its entrance way is marked by Murchison Drive.

For the rest of the mansions we turn southward, for north of Millbrae they did not go, unless we include the Charles Lux home in the South San Francisco area, which ended its days humbly, serving as a house for Miller-and-Lux foremen.

South of the San Mateo group, near the present Barneson Avenue, the Whipple stock farm was bought in 1884 by W. S. Hobart, who built a substantial home there. In the 1890's it passed into the hands of Charles W. Clark, son of the famous copper king. His widow, Mrs. Tobin Clark, still lives (1963) in her House on Hill on a westerly portion of the property. The lower portion is now completely urbanized and the city is rapidly climbing into the hills. A piece of the estate is now on College Heights, forming a portion of the new College of San Mateo campus.

Still farther south, during the hard times of the 1870's, Antoine Borel, San Francisco banker and later consul for Switzerland, bought from the bankrupt estate of F. L. A. Pioche a large tract of land on which he built his home and surrounded it with elaborate landscaping. His house was large, featuring high ceilings, and was furnished in the grand manner, but in architecture and size it was not to be compared with those of Hayward and Mills. Rather, his special love was lavished on his gardens and grounds. There was a planted forest of trees, concealing neatly trimmed lawns, grottoes and ponds, ornamental bridges, and winding walks and driveways.

To his large family of children, who grew up on this place between frequent visits to Switzerland, Mr. Borel was the stern but loving *pater familias,* European style. Eventually, there was a residence near-by for his only son, Antoine Jr., and on the immediate grounds were homes for his two married daughters, Mrs. Aylett R. Cotton and Mrs. Louis Bovet.

A landmark on the edge of the estate, facing El Camino Real, was the small Geneva Chapel, which is said to have been built partly as a family chapel and partly for an incipient Presbyterian congregation. But the Presbyterian effort did not succeed, and the chapel was later acquired by the Congregational Church of San Mateo, then by the Episcopal Church of St. Matthew. Finally, it served for 17 years as the Hillbarn Theater, operated by the Peninsula Little Theater group. It was demolished in December, 1961, to make way for the 19th Avenue Freeway.

A tradition of the early years was the annual Christmas party held in the Geneva Chapel, patterned after a similar custom in Switzerland. Children of the neighborhood were encouraged to make their wants known to Santa Claus by writing him care of the Borels. The party was managed by the Borel girls, so that each child got just what he wanted. The party became a symbol of the Borel family's generosity and attachment to the community—although separated in some measure by difference in wealth, they were not aloof from their neighbors.

When the railroad had drawn the Peninsula together and brought its most distant Bayside sectors close to San Francisco, Menlo Park soon followed San Mateo in becoming a center for country mansions. Some time in the 1850's, two young Irishmen had named their farm Menlo Park, and to make no mistake about it, had erected a sign announcing the fact on arches over their gates. Being fresh from Menlough, County Galway of the Old Sod, and their wives being sisters, they erected two houses with a common driveway, and over the entrance a high arch that bore the words MENLO (August, 1852) PARK. On either side was a smaller arch, one bearing the name D. J. Oliver and the other D. C. McGlynn.

This landmark suggested to the railroad people the placing of a Menlo Park station across the road from it. The roadside sign stood until July 7, 1922 when it was knocked down by an automobile, but the quaint little railroad station, erected as its visual echo in the early 1860's, still stands with its outward appearance unchanged though it is now the office of the local chamber of commerce instead of the railroad.

Oliver and McGlynn were apparently having land trouble of some kind. This may have been the reason for the sign—an item in the rough play of pressures and

Millbrae, home of Darius Ogden Mills.

FAMILY CIRCLE on the porch of the new Mills mansion, 1870. Seated left to right: Mrs. D. O. Mills, an unnamed governess, Mrs. Ansel I. Easton (Adeline Mills), Mrs. Edward Taylor (Fanny Easton). Standing left: Jenny Easton (Mrs. Fred Crocker). Standing right: Elizabeth Mills (Mrs. Whitelaw Reid).

rivalries for land titles. Whatever the game was, they seem to have been the losers for, despite the long-standing sign, there is no official record of their ever having secured title to the farm on which it stood.

However, around the station a village began to grow, and around the village the level, oak-studded farms were bought up by agents and subdividers who turned them into villa lots or country estates. In the course of a decade or so these estates were spread out on the map from the Stanford farm on the south to the Athertons and Selbys on the north. Later, the more northerly of these estates obtained a railroad station of their own called Fair Oaks, now Atherton.

When Faxon Dean Atherton decided to bring his family from Chile to California, his purchase of 500 acres on El Camino Real at the present Atherton Avenue intersection was only one of several investments in California land. This one was planned for a summer home; in the rainy season country roads were impassable and, furthermore, his large family, coming directly from the Chilean aristocracy, would want to be in San Francisco for the social season.

The house he built in the center of the tract, now the site of the Menlo Circus Club, was almost stark in its plainness—a square, two-story, substantial-looking structure, with just enough ornamentation to give it dignity, matching the rather formal and solid conservatism that was characteristic of the family.

Faxon D., himself, became one of the county's most substantial citizens and a leader in south-county development. Five of his children, as they grew up, established homes locally: Elena (Mrs. Frank Macondray, who after the death of her first husband became Mrs. Percy Selby); Alejandra (Mrs. Lawrence Rathbone); and Florence (Mrs. E. S. Eyre). Faxon Jr. married Jennie Selby, and George married Gertrude Franklin who, under the name of Gertrude Atherton, achieved fame as one of California's most prolific writers (fifty books), much to the chagrin of the rest of the Athertons, particularly because of the sensational nature of her earliest productions.

Thomas H. Selby, prominent industrialist in the smelting of precious metals and one-time Mayor of San Francisco, bought land joining the Athertons' on the north and extending to the present Selby Lane. Mr. Selby was able to enjoy his country place only a few years, for he died in 1875. His house, on Almendral Avenue, including all its valuable contents, was destroyed by fire in 1884.

One of the most glamorous houses in the southern area was on the wide stretch of land between San Francisquito Creek and Ravenswood Avenue, from El Camino to Middlefield Road. The first large home erected here was by W. E. Barron, one of the principal owners of the New Almaden mercury mine near San José; but about 1872 it was purchased by United States Senator Milton S. Latham, who had just sold his railroad (Sacramento to Vallejo) to the Central Pacific Company. He had also just acquired a young bride to help him spend his money, which she apparently did rather effectively.

It seems that in the course of remodeling the Barron house it took fire and burned, and the Lathams then built in its place the mansion that was later named

Sherwood Hall—a house with towers and balustrades befitting in size and dignity a rich man's bride.

The Lathams loved to entertain in the grand manner. From the record set down by a Menlo Park old-timer with a memory for details, these are the vehicles that came at one time to meet their guests at the train: a guest wagon for baggage and trunks; a guest bus holding about seven people and drawn by two snow-white horses; a tally-ho with two dapple greys; a basket vehicle behind a Shetland stallion driven for two children; and a sulky wagon drawn by two Shetland ponies.

It would seem that neither Latham nor his fortune were equal to this pace of living, for by 1883, he was dead and his estate bankrupt. The estate was then purchased by the Hopkins family. Mark Hopkins, treasurer of his company and one of the Big Four who built the Central Pacific Railroad, was now dead and his adopted son, Timothy Hopkins, had taken over his job; the company was now the Southern Pacific and its policies were being guided mainly by Collis P. Huntington.

Timothy Hopkins, a man of simple tastes like his foster father, tall and quietly efficient in the handling of company business as well as his own interests, had married Clara Crittendon, niece of his foster mother, and it was he and Clara who now took up residence in the former Latham place. The home became Sherwood Hall, after the family name of Clara's mother and of her aunt, Mrs. Mark Hopkins.

Timothy was a regular commuter to his office in San Francisco, but he also took part in community affairs as a member of the Menlo Park District school board. Sherwood Hall was so badly damaged by the earthquake of 1906 that it was never repaired and the couple thereafter lived, when on the estate, in a cottage on Ravenswood Avenue. Timothy died in 1936 and Clara in 1941.

Sherwood Hall remained abandoned and forlorn in the field until World War II; the furnishings were then sold to a Hollywood motion picture company and the building demolished to make way for the Army's Dibble Hospital. The property was willed to Stanford University.

Leland Stanford, Ex-Governor of California and later United States Senator, besides being one of the Big Four railroad combination, had bought the Gordon farm in the edge of Santa Clara County, added a vast acreage to it and had begun there to indulge his taste for racehorses. While there, the Stanfords lived in the house that is now a part of the Stanford Convalescent Home for children. It was then a richly furnished country house.

Hundreds of horses were trained here, and as a device for studying the leg movements of a running horse, the first steps in the invention of motion pictures were taken on Stanford's Palo Alto Farm. Later, after the death of his only son, Leland Jr., a portion of the vast farm became the campus of Leland Stanford Jr. Memorial University. Though the Stanford farm headquarters were across the county line, Menlo Park was the family's nearest railway station and they were regarded as a part of the Menlo Park community.

James C. Flood, probably because he suffered keenly in childhood from the chagrin of being poor, developed a driving determination to become rich. He succeeded so well that, by age 45, he was enjoying an income of $250,000 a month.

Achievement so great and so rare as this is bound to inspire at least two questions about the man who made it: How did he do it, and what use did he make of the money when he got it?

These questions are inspired by more than mere idle curiosity. All the world is interested in human achievement and the magnitude of it is never fully measured by the size of a bank account or by the smart techniques employed in acquiring it. Just as important is the true caliber of the man, as shown by his code of ethics in building a large fortune and his poise in the possession and the spending of it.

In his early efforts at money-making, Mr. Flood met with some failures, one of which was in the San Francisco panic of 1855. From this defeat he took a lesson and looked around for the kind of business that would be least affected by depressions, and decided he would sell liquor. He observed, as others have done, that people, when times were hard, drank anyway—perhaps even more than when times were good. With a partner, William S. O'Brien, he opened a saloon in San Francisco which happened to be near the Mining Exchange, where stocks of the Comstock mines were bought and sold.

When the brokers came in for a drink, Flood listened carefully to their conversation and found that, with the tips and innuendos he gathered, he could play the market successfully. So successful he was, in fact, that Flood and O'Brien were soon no longer eavesdropping saloon keepers but stock brokers, and then bonanza mine owners.

But what does one do with the kind of income Flood found himself receiving? Especially one who was born to labor—who instead of being sent to school was apprenticed, at an early age, to a carriage maker? How can one handle such sums of money so as to derive from it the satisfactions that wealth is supposed to bring? While working and scheming for wealth chiefly because he abhorred poverty, had Jim Flood thought of this?

Apparently he had. At least he did not go to either of the extremes that novices at being rich often take; he was neither a miser nor a spendthrift. In the inevitable battles between the giants of finance he handled himself successfully under a code of ethics that was, at least, as virtuous as that of his adversaries; and while he fought off the equally inevitable army of panhandlers, and refused to spoil people with gifts, he proved that he was not entirely lacking in generosity. Not a few young men were fitted out by him with blocks of promising stocks and guided in the right use of them so as to earn a financial start in life; and in gifts to charities and other causes he was not niggardly or mean. He did not endow a college or a hospital, nor did he set up a fund for the better education of poor men's sons. If he had, he would have been living ahead of his times. Not even the Carnegies or the Rockefellers had developed this kind of social conscience in his day.

In his own use of his money James Flood took the natural course—just what others were doing with it. The thing to do at the time was to build not only a mansion in San Francisco but also a country home down the Peninsula, and since he commanded financial power even beyond the dreams of most wealthy men, his mansion

Coach and Four arriving at Carolan Polo Field, Burlingame.

Polo enthusiasts watching game at Carolan Clubhouse.

William H. Crocker's home, New Place, is now the Burlingame Country Club. Photographs below show him as a concerned child and carefree adult.

117

Harriet Pullman Carolan and her nationally-known Chateau in Hillsborough.

should not fail to fit the station in life that he had achieved. It should be the visible and unmistakable assertion of his real superiority.

He bought for this purpose a farm on Middlefield Road, to which he added later purchases to make a total of about 600 acres, and proceeded to build there his idea of a really magnificent country estate. It was indeed magnificent, despite a good deal of critical comment. It was called "Flood's wedding cake", its massive expanse of whiteness affected one man "like the playing of a brass band", while another called it a "beautiful atrocity", referring no doubt to its great variety of adornment.

Three stories high, this masterpiece of carpenter's Gothic was surmounted by a tower the equivalent of three stories more, besides many lesser towers, ornamental chimneys, and other upward projections, plus delicately carved fancy work that gave a feathery touch like the frosting on a cake. Art critics got in their jibes but no one denied its magnificence or its beauty. Appropriately, it was called Linden Towers.

Built of the most expensive materials, it was finished inside with rare and precious woods from all parts of the world, and fitted with draperies and furniture to match its grandeur. Its setting was among the oak trees of the Menlo Park flats, surrounded by a great expanse of lawns and curving driveways.

Most owners of country mansions set great store by their stables, featuring stalls finished in rare woods, silver mounted harness, and fine horses. All this Flood had, too, plus especially fine carriages, for he knew the best in carriages when he saw them.

James C. Flood did not have long to enjoy his Linden Towers for he died in 1889, and his white castle was inherited by his unmarried daughter, Jennie. She, in turn, made it a gift to the University of California. But the University soon found that the gift was a white elephant, with heavy expense and no income, and that sagacious institution persuaded the son, James L. Flood, to buy it back for sentimental reasons, to keep it in the family. It was used by him intermittently until his death in 1926.

In the end, the Flood mansion faced the dilemma that sooner or later confronts all such buildings: no use could be found for it that would justify the heavy cost of taxes and upkeep. Finally, in 1934, the furniture was sold at auction and the rare structure that had been built to last forever, but was scarcely fifty years old, was demolished. Its site is now covered with new ranch-type homes.

Bordering the Floods on the south was the home of Joseph A. Donohoe, member of the San Francisco banking firm of Donohoe, Kelly & Co., who built his country home in 1868. His son, Joseph Jr., married Christine Parrott of San Mateo, and John Parrott Jr., in turn, married the younger Donohoe's sister. The site of the home is now a part of the Menlo-Atherton High School campus.

Around the corner from Donohoe on Oak Grove Avenue was the home of John T. Doyle, also built in 1868. Doyle was in his time one of California's most famous attorneys, and he accumulated in his home a library that was reputed to be the best in California. His place is also now a part of the Menlo-Atherton High School campus.

One of the best-known places over a period of years was Felton Gables, the home of Charles N. Felton. As a United States Treasury official in San Francisco and as United States Senator, Felton was a familiar figure in the Bay Area, and at his home he entertained, from time to time, such personages as Prince Edward of Wales (later King Edward VII), General U. S. Grant, and President Benjamin Harrison.

Also worthy of mention are the homes of Edward Hopkins, distant relative of Timothy, of Edgar Mills, brother of D. O. Mills of Millbrae; of Mrs. Kate Johnson, which is now the campus of St. Patrick's Seminary; and Elmwood, built in 1875 by Charles Holbrook and the life-long home of his daughter, Mrs. Silas H. Palmer. This house, on Watkins Avenue, burned in 1957 with all of its priceless contents of antique furniture and other possessions that had been in the house from its beginning.

Most of the wealthy men's estates were grouped around San Mateo and Menlo Park, but not all. At Redwood City lived Horace Hawes, where now the campus of Sequoia High School is located. Hawes accumulated a fortune by his own efforts, and once owned a vast tract of land reaching from Edgewood Road to Five Points and from El Camino back into the hills. His daughter, Caroline, was married to James A. Robinson, son of Alfredo Robinson, the early California pioneer and author of the well-known book, *Life in California*. The Robinsons lived in the same house, and close neighbor to them was another famous name, Moses Hopkins, brother of the more famous Mark Hopkins.

For another group of well-known families the charm of Woodside was irresistible, though, prior to automobile days, a home there meant almost complete retirement from the rest of the world. Nevertheless, in 1883 banker John A. Hooper bought the large Mountain Home Ranch (Charles Brown Adobe) and went there to live. He, and each of his children after him, built a handsome and comfortable home on the property, and they have carefully maintained the historic adobe.

Other famous names that long ago graced the Woodside-Searsville-Portola Valley are C. F. A. Talbot of Pope & Talbot, lumber dealers; Daniel Jackling inventor of a new copper-smelting process; J. A. Folger (coffee); August Schilling (spices); and Charles Josselyn, owner of a ship chandlery business in San Francisco.

The valley is still known as a place for homes of wealthy men and, in order to keep it in this category, the people of the valley voted in 1956 to incorporate a city of Woodside, not, in fact, because they want to be a city but rather to keep from being one.

By the turn of the century, the era of great mansions seemed to have died, at least this was so by 1906 when the San Francisco earthquake and fire started masses of middle-class people moving into towns on the Peninsula. But like a late, off-season crop of blooms on rose bushes, the hills of the Peninsula blossomed forth once more with a few new and fabulous dwellings. Already most of the Victorian estates had slid into a quiet oblivion, and a mushrooming row of commuter towns was springing up along the lines of transportation. So rapidly were the towns of San Mateo and Burlingame annexing territory that the town of Hillsborough was incorporated (1910) as a means of defense for the group that had created the exclusive Burlingame Country Club.

Perhaps it was this city of refuge for the wealthy that suggested to the Crockers and the Carolans that here was a good place to do some extraordinary building. Already there was the Crocker Skyfarm tucked away in a hidden canyon. Now William H. Crocker planned and built his fabulous New Place which has recently been sold to the Country Club, and Charles Templeton Crocker planned his Uplands.

The latter, Italian in style, was designed by the famous American architect, Willis Polk. It is large but not huge—roughly 100 by 200 feet and 40 feet high—with proportional arrangement of mass and height that fits the hilltop surroundings and gives a feeling of stability. It is solidly constructed of steel, concrete, and brick. Inside the halls are massive, cold, and beautiful, albeit their present use as a girls' school seems more fitting than as a substitute for the warmth and comfort of a home, just as New Place in these times fits more appropriately its role as a club house.

The most spectacular of the later mansions was the brain child of Harriet Pullman Carolan, heiress to a share of the vast parlor car fortune of George M. Pullman. While she and her husband, Francis Carolan, were active members of the Burlingame Country Club set, she conceived the idea of an imposing mansion atop the highest hill in Hillsborough.

She bought 554.32 acres of land and engaged four French architects to submit plans. Her four-story *chateau* of upwards of 92 rooms was built of concrete and brick and finished inside with grand staircases, massive wrought-iron banisters and gold leaf trimmings. For a portion of it, rooms were lifted bodily from a *chateau* in France and built into her mansion. The hilly land around it was leveled in broad terraces and, in imitation of European castles, adorned with statuary and a Temple of Love. Barns and dairy cows for the outer portions were contemplated to make the place self-sustaining. It was said some forty employees were needed to operate the place, divided about equally between "outside and inside".

But most of these ambitions were never realized. The distractions of the First World War intervened; then Harriet and Francis separated, and after his death in 1923 the furnishings were put in storage and the place abandoned. It has since been purchased and refurnished by the Countess Lillian Remillard Dandini, a native of the Bay Area who was married to an Italian count, and who enjoys living in it despite her taste, in other respects, for simple living. It stands alone on a five-acre remnant of the original estate, the rest having been subdivided and sold for modern homes.

A quiet *finis* to the age of mansions was written in 1916 by the philosopher-president of the Spring Valley Water Company, Mr. W. B. Bourn. On a reserved portion of his company's vast watershed, in the valley of the lakes, he built his retreat—a place remote and peaceful, but also elegant. For a name, he combined what to him were three of the most important words in the language—fidelity, love, life—and came up with FILOLI.

Under titles like "Thoughts on Character", Mr. Bourn wrote articles for his company's periodical, *San Francisco Water,* with quotes from Goethe and

Browning. "In a period of serene contentment", he commented, "while an empire was making ready to pour another unlimited stream of wealth into her lap, the soul of San Francisco was developing."

His mansion of brick and tile, planned by Willis Polk, reflects this search for a soul, as well as the "constructive conservatism" that he advocated. It covered something like 18,000 square feet of ground space, and rose in its main section to the height of two stories plus a basement and attic. And according to documents in the files of the San Mateo County Historical Association, he built it, with the powerful dollars of his day, including everything from carpentry to marble work, for $109,308.

In recent years it has been the home of Mr. and Mrs. William P. Roth, who historically have been associated with the Matson Navigation Company and its famous "White Ships".

If this were Europe, these wealthy Peninsula dwellers would probably have been called the landed gentry, but for various reasons the term does not fit here. Americans, especially in the West, abhor the idea of social classes. But Americans do make social distinctions based on wealth, and in the Victorian era these were more pronounced than in recent times. The top business and professional men, here as well as in Europe, were then expected to dress in a manner befitting their success in life; the Prince Albert coat was a respected badge of distinction. (Senator Stanford even wore his to a Belmont picnic!)

But habits of dress have changed in the direction of more democracy, and huge mansions, too, have gone out of style. There are no fewer wealthy people today on the Peninsula, and many of their homes are still objects of community pride. But the life of the wealthier people has become urban, sophisticated, and self-sufficient; they tend to seek anonymity rather than public notice.

The era of the great estates, which is now history, brought to the Peninsula something more than glamor. The expenditures necessary to the maintenance of the mansions, grounds, and stables, to say nothing of the living expenses, furnished a large share of the economic sinews of the villages that served them. Now that the entire Peninsula is becoming urbanized, it is noteworthy that some of the former estates have served another useful purpose; their land has been kept out of the hands of subdividers until the day of zoning and city planning. The communities can now control their own development with a minimum of blighted areas to deal with. One regrettable fact is that more of the park-like grounds of these estates, as well as some of the more distinctive buildings, have not been spared for public use and enjoyment.

It seems, too, that San Mateo families of means and leisure had something to do with pointing the way to today's era of emphasis on "living"—now called "gracious" living, also "outdoor", or "Western" living. Leisure now is no longer thought of as the exclusive privilege of a class, and the conveniences that were once luxuries for the few have become necessities of the many. In terms of physical comforts and happy environment these conditions add up to the highest level of living ever achieved by mankind, and this Peninsula, without doubt, has held, and still offers, the most ideal kind of conditions for such achievement.

Does all this lead to the "good life" in any higher sense? Or does it perhaps have a retarding influence? Time, perhaps, will tell us—if we have the wit to interpret the answers as they are given.

Pigeon Point Light, watchtower of the Coastside since 1872.

# VII. The Coastsiders: *in quest of an outlet*

*"The history of human society is the history of man's progressive struggle with his environment."*     BLAKE ROSS

James Johnston fell in love with the Coastside, particularly the open country around Half Moon Bay, and was determined to live there—even though to get into that secluded region one had either to walk or ride a horse. Up to his time (1853) no wheeled vehicles had ever been maneuvered over the steep hills.

Pablo Vásquez, who lived there in Johnston's time, wrote a story that gives us an idea how serious a barrier those hills were. His father, Tiburcio, he said, so admired American wagons when he first saw them that he paid $400 to get one for his Coastside rancho. He was given full instructions on how to get down a steep hill by tying a wheel to make it slide,—or if the hill was very steep, by tying two wheels. He followed instructions, but unacquainted as he was with wagon dynamics, instead of tying the two rear wheels, he tied a front wheel and a back one, on the same side. The result was a grand spill that strewed the contents of his wagon over the hillside.

There was no easy way either around or over this barrier of hills. In those days, the Peninsula's central ridge, and its two high projections that reach out like the points of a crescent to touch the sea, virtually shut off a large section of Coastside territory from any contact, except on horseback, with the rest of the Peninsula. *The north projection was the high Montara (San Pedro) Mountain that ended in a cliff and the Devil's Slide, and the south point of the crescent was the chalk-soft ridge, now the county's southern boundary line, that also extended to the beach, where the tides lapped at the foot of its crumbling slope. This southerly point could be by-passed if one were traveling via Santa Cruz but, even then, only by waiting for low tide so as to travel on the wet sand.

---

*Antonino Buelna opened a road to his Rancho San Gregorio, from his other land grant on the present site of Stanford University. This was later referred to as a wagon road, but in Buelna's time wagons were not known here. Probably in rancho days his road was navigated, though precariously, by oxcarts.

Johnston came from San Francisco, but he would not be stopped by small barriers like hills. The land he had bought from Candelario Miramontes, lying near Pilarcitos Creek and sloping gently toward the sea, was indeed attractive and, having married a Spanish woman, he no doubt felt that he had something in common with the Spanish-speaking people in the neighboring village of San Benito.

This village of perhaps 75 people, where now stands the town of Half Moon Bay, had come into being in the previous five or six years as a by-product of the war between the United States and Mexico (1846-1848). The American armed forces had occupied California without encountering serious resistance, but there had been warlike tensions and incidents of hostility that caused people, particularly the native Californians, to seek the seclusion of out-of-the-way places.

Hostilities in this war began unofficially with the Bear Flag uprising, but the first local war-time shock came when Captain John C. Fremont's party, encamped at Mission San Rafael, shot down three men as they landed from a small boat on the Marin shore. They were assumed to be carrying messages to the enemy. Two of the men killed were the young de Haro twins of Rancho Lake Merced, grandsons of José Sánchez, and the third was their uncle, José Berryesa. Their frightened family moved into a crowded house in a ravine that no longer exists, remote from the public highway, near Lake Merced Boulevard.

Some six months later came another incident, one that concerned nearly everybody on the Peninsula. Fremont and other American authorities, finding difficulty in obtaining food for the armed forces and for the increasing civilian population of San Francisco, had resorted to the practice of seizing cattle from the rancho herds, giving in payment their informal promissory notes which depended for their real value on a future act of Congress.

When this practice became so general as to be a serious matter for the rancheros, Francisco Sánchez, commander of the local Mexican militia company and one of the heavy losers of cattle, decided to make a gesture of resistance. When Washington Bartlett, Alcalde of San Francisco, came down the Peninsula after cattle, Sánchez rode over from his rancho in San Pedro Valley with a posse of Californians, met Bartlett near the present San Bruno, and took him prisoner.

As Fremont, with all the volunteers he could muster, had gone to southern California, it was now the Americans' turn to be frightened, and the Californians rallied to Sánchez' side—reportedly mustering about a hundred men. The situation was tense but, for about three weeks, the Americans, lacking military personnel, did nothing to rescue Bartlett.

Finally, a mixed company with a field cannon, under Captain Ward Marston of the United States Marines, set out from San Francisco toward Santa Clara where Sánchez had lately put in an appearance, seemingly in a movement against San José.

As the *Yanquis* approached Santa Clara, Sánchez and his men attacked them in a running skirmish, using the tactic commonly practiced by the Californians (all exceedingly clever horsemen) of dashing up to fire a volley, then, as quickly, riding out of range. Despite so-called eye-witness accounts of fierce fighting, the most reliable reports say there were no casualties except, possibly, two Americans slightly wounded. But Sánchez retired to the hills. There is some evidence that he, too, had a cannon, and the recent discovery of a three-inch gun on the former Rolph Ranch south of Portola Valley tends to confirm it.

That evening, Sánchez sent a party to the *gringos* under a flag of truce, offering to surrender under certain conditions, the conditions supposedly having to do with the matter of seizing cattle. Officially, no conditions were accepted, but with the good offices of the British Consul, James Alexander Forbes, the matter was settled; Sánchez surrendered and was later released, with unofficial assurances that property rights would be respected. Bartlett was delivered up, unharmed.

These incidents explain the sudden appearance of a Spanish-speaking village on the remote and more secure Coastside. This village, called San Benito after the official name of Miramontes' rancho, was later dubbed Spanishtown by the Americans. It began with Candelario Miramontes and Tiburcio Vásquez who, in 1840, had received their two grants on opposite sides of Pilarcitos Creek, but had operated them as absentee landlords. Now, to avoid trouble with the Americans, they moved their families there and were soon followed by kinfolk and friends.

A contractor had brought in a crew of captive Indian laborers from the Tulare country in the San Joaquin Valley to build seven adobe-brick houses. So isolated was this village at that time that even the Gold Rush had no effect on it, until after 1853. Then more Mexicans and many Chilean immigrants moved in.

Then it was also that James Johnston, having bought the southerly half of Miramontes' rancho, while his brothers brought out cattle and supplies from Ohio, undertook to build his house. He would show those rancheros in their little adobe structures what a good American farmhouse could be like. It took some doing and considerable expense. Hauling lumber over the hill was out of the question, so he brought it in by ship, boldly dumping it in the sea and picking it up again like driftwood on the beach.

His house still stands in its commanding position south of Half Moon Bay, overlooking the coast highway and the ocean—but with nothing about it to suggest the stylish life it housed in the days of James and his aristocratic wife, Petra, or, after Petra's untimely death, with grandmother, Melita, and James' sister Isabel.

In those times Chinese servants served tea in a richly furnished Victorian parlor. There were tables and chests of rare oriental wood with inlaid mother-of-pearl, and draperies of lace and brocade that hung at the windows, with little bells that tinkled and harps that sang when stirred by breezes from the sea. Today (1963) the breezes blow unhindered through gaping holes where the windows used to be. Bulldozers e'er long will push the old house over and clear the ground for the building of an expanding city.

When the Johnston brothers arrived with their cattle and supplies from the East, they had their turn at the tricky business of getting heavily loaded wagons down the steep hill, but they had learned, on the trail of the Forty Niners, how to do it. The family tradition has it that seven of their eight wagons got down safely but the eighth one upset, which strongly suggests that they used the windlass method made memorable by Windlass Hill on the famous trans-Sierra trail to California.

The trick was to use one of the wagons as a windlass by tying it firmly to stakes driven into the ground, with one wheel jacked up to turn freely. The end of a long rope was then attached to the rear of another wagon, and a turn of the rope taken around the hub of this free wheel. With one or more men holding the rope and others the wheel, that free wheel became a windlass that eased the wagons one by one down the hill. And what about the windlass wagon? This, with the Johnstons, was the one that upset!

Two years more elapsed before the County of San Francisco, of which the Peninsula was still a part, graded the semblance of a road over the mountains from San Mateo (1855), and another along the coast from Pedro or Montara Mountain to Tunitas Creek where Santa Cruz County then began—at least so said Santa Cruz. Not until 1866 was there a good road over the mountains and then it was a privately-built toll road.

While the Johnstons were settling at Half Moon Bay, a similar entry was being made at the south end of the Coastside crescent. Alexander Moore, who had come with a wagon train from Missouri to California two years before the Gold Rush, and had settled at Santa Cruz, was the first American settler at Pescadero. His belongings and lumber for his house were hauled from Santa Cruz, by-passing the chalk mountain on the wet beach, and up to the spot where his house still stands (1963), in good condition, a short distance from the present town. He also built the first school house and paid the teacher, largely for his own children who constituted most of the student body.

By 1860, Pescadero was a prosperous village surrounded by farms, and in 1862 the Steele Brothers began, farther south, the setting up of a chain of dairies for operation on a large scale.

On the Coastside as a whole, during the 1850's dozens of others moved in, some to buy land, some as renters and some as squatters. Like all settlers on a new frontier, they had to be gamblers of a sort. They gambled whatever money they had, and years of hard work, on the chance that they could feed themselves while getting a start, and that, ultimately, a way would be found to get their surplus products out to a market.

There was no lack of resources—good farm and grazing land, and redwood timber in the recesses of the canyons. But this was rough country. The road that finally made its snake-like way the length of the Coastside crescent skirted rounding hillsides and dipped deep into the gorges that had to be crossed. Connected with the toll road over the lowest pass to San Mateo, it brought stagecoach service that carried mail and passengers through dust or mud with remarkable regularity. But to haul the heavy products of farm and sawmill over the 800-foot hill was slow and the cost was prohibitive.

The alternative outlet was the sea. In the sheltered bay behind Pillar Point, small ships could anchor safely and men could wade out to the boats with bags of grain on their shoulders. By 1858 a wharf reached out to deep water, and in 1868 Josiah P. Ames built another at Miramar (then Amesport) that saved two or three miles of hauling for the farmers toward the south. Ships tied up at these wharves to load grain, baled hay, and potatoes for San Francisco.

But for the farmers on the south end of the long and hilly coast road, this shipping point was out of reach. Their first answer to the problem was to concentrate on dairying, putting out only the most easily transported products: butter and cheese. By Civil-War time this business had so far developed that the Steeles, one of whose brothers was a general in the Union Army, gained wide fame by making, from one day's milk, a single giant cheese that weighed two tons. Given for the benefit of the Sanitary Service (the Red Cross of that day), it was sold at auction in San Francisco for a dollar a pound, and a sample was sent to President Lincoln.

But the south Coastside would not forever limit itself to making butter and cheese. There was lumber in the canyons, and high prices were demanding that it be brought out. Also, a variety of farm products wanted only a means of transportation to make them profitable. Perhaps because a number of the settlers had come from the "stern and rockbound coast" of New England, they managed to find a way.

Point Año Nuevo was no harbor, but the point itself and its off-shore island did shelter a piece of ocean from the northwest wind. Here a roving reporter from San Francisco's *Alta California,* found, in 1867, a wharf 700 feet long high above the surf, from which bundles of shingles were sent by a slide to the decks of schooners. This daring dock was connected by a wooden railroad with Waddell's shingle mill five miles away. There was also a mill on Whitehouse Creek that was sending shingles, lumber, and tan oak to the same port. The latter product, worth twenty-five dollars a cord, was shipped through the Golden Gate and around to the tanneries in Redwood City.

Under the lee side of Pigeon Point was a similar anchorage—a place where ships could be warped into a space not much bigger than a drydock, provided the weather remained calm. According to Col. Albert S. Evans, who wrote in 1869 for the far-away New York *Tribune,* "Out about 200 yards from the shore is a high monument-like rock, rising to a level with the steep rock bluff which encloses the bay. From the bluff to the top of this rock stretches a heavy wire cable, kept taut by a capstan. A vessel rounding the reef runs into the sheltered cove under this hawser, and casts anchor. Slings running down the hawser are rigged, and her cargo lifted from the deck, load by load, run up into the air 50 to 100 feet, then hauled in shore, and landed upon the top of the bluff. Lumber, hay in bales like cotton, fruit, potatoes, vegetables, dairy products, etc., etc., are in like manner run out and lowered at the right moment upon the vessel's decks. If a south-wester comes on she slips her anchor and runs out to sea until it is over."

Other variations of these loading processes were experimented with from time to time—even a simple hawser stretched from a post high on a headland to the rigging of a ship anchored in the open sea a safe distance from shore—safe, that is, as long as the sea was calm. Down this hawser, slings on a pulley carried freight to the deck of the ship.

Down the hill now scarred by an early road, the Johnston Brothers lowered wagons by the windlass method. (Below) Levy Brothers' stage and store, Pescadero.

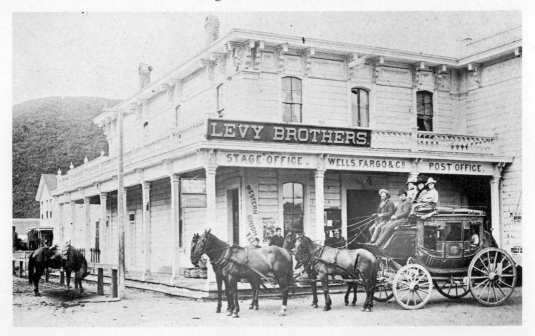

Gordon's Chute, built in 1872, was a Coastsider's most daring attempt to build a port. (Below) Hazards of steamer loading at Pigeon Point.

The most daring attempt of all to create a port where nature had provided none was the famous Gordon's Chute. Alexander Gordon had a thousand-acre farm on Tunitas Creek and, influenced by the success of shipping at Pigeon Point and Año Nuevo, he conceived the idea of a chute from the high bluff at Tunitas which faced the open sea. Such a device, situated midway between Pigeon Point and the wharves at Half Moon Bay, would not only solve his own shipping problem but it would also profitably serve the farms and lumber mills of the entire central Coastside.

The framework of his structure was built on rocks awash in the sea, visible only at low tide, at the foot of a hundred-foot bluff. The chute, down which the cargo was to slide, ran at an angle of about 45 degrees from the top of the cliff to an apron at the bottom that could be swung down to the deck of the ship. The goods to be loaded had only to be taken from the warehouse at the top and started down the chute—gravity would do the rest.

The thing looked grand but there was trouble from the start. First, the friction of the long slide burned holes in the bags of grain and potatoes, or they burst with the impact of hitting the deck. The worst obstacle was the reluctance of ship captains to come to this hazardous seacliff, which required nothing short of braving the swells of the open ocean to tie up to a reef. Obviously, loading could be carried on only in the fairest of weather. With no shelter at all, if the wind rose from any direction the ship had to drop her moorings and put out to sea.

Gordon also had the bad luck of having started his enterprise in 1872, on the eve of a nation-wide financial panic and a long depression. With all of this against it, the chute stood idle for long periods of time, produce spoiled in the warehouse, and the enterprise went bankrupt. Finally the sea did its inevitable work of undermining the chute itself and a storm in 1885 left it a complete wreck. Nothing remains of it now but the eye-bolts in the rocks that supported it.

But while shipping difficulties were hampering certain kinds of growth, people of the Coastside did not fail to find other things to do. To the surprise of many, even the settlers themselves, Pescadero in the 1860's began to gather fame as a summer resort. Mrs. Charles Swanton, wife of a blacksmith, started a trend by supplying lodging for hunters and fishermen, and in a few years found herself operating a hotel that was known far and wide as the Swanton House.

Not only did San Franciscans tell each other about the place, but displaced New Englanders wrote to their friends across the continent, with the result that by 1884, *Appleton's General Guide to the United States and Canada* listed under "California Resorts", PESCADERO (Swanton's Hotel)".

It was reached by stage, said the *Guide,* "from San Mateo or Redwood City on the Southern Pacific R.R. The stage ride of thirty miles over the Contra Costa (sic) Range affords some noble views. Pescadero is a thriving town, beautifully situated in a remarkably productive valley, on both sides of Pescadero Creek, near its confluence with the Butano, about a mile from the sea-shore. - - - Near the town is the famous *Pebble Beach,* where agates, opals, jaspers, and carnelians, of almost every conceivable color, are found in great abundance, with a natural polish imparted by the action of the waves."

Except for a slip in the name of the mountains, the description was quite accurate, and judging by a report in the *Alta California* (May, 1867), Pebble Beach, to which the hotel guests were taken by the wagon load each morning to spend the day, was indeed the resort's greatest asset.

"The whole conversation at the hotel", said the writer, "is pebbles. The house is full of them; one steps on them in the parlor or on the stairs; visitors carry them in their pockets and compare them at the breakfast table; they are, in fact, in *everybody's mouth!* I verily believe they carry them to bed, and dream of pebbles all night - - - ."

At the beach, he went on, "they pass the day buried up in pebbles. - - - From the cliff above a full view of the scene may be had, which is ludicrous in the extreme. Imagine a dozen females, some in bloomers, and some *without;* some with long, some with short dresses, high boots and low-cut gaiters, straw hats, green veils, bandanas, and the inevitable Shaker—lying about in every conceivable position, some on the knees and hands, others flat on their stomachs, with hands busy, feet stretched out, and heads half buried in holes they have made in the beach. - - - Were there but some wreck in sight it would have the appearance of a number of bodies washed up by the waves - - - ." Looking more closely under one of the Shaker bonnets, the reporter found "a well known face of a lady from San Francisco who wears her silks and fine bonnets there."

A very different sort of industry was also able to flourish on the isolated Coastside, which our friend Col. Evans discovered while on a horseback tour of the sights. On the Pigeon Point headland, where now stands the towering lighthouse, were a dozen cottages that housed the families of Portuguese whalers.

"As we rode up", he wrote, "two long, sharp, single-masted boats, with odd-looking sails, shot out to sea. On the point, by the side of flag staffs, on which signals were to be hoisted to guide the boats in their pursuit, crouched two of the party with their sea glasses, intently watching the boats and sweeping the horizon. - - - One of the signal men could speak a little English (?). 'E blow! e blow! One close herd starboard boat! Carraho, now he run! Ze son of seacook, how he run; dam a he! Believe myself he get away!' Then carried away by his feelings, he proceeded to curse in good Portuguese, honestly and squarely, for fifteen minutes, and I felt my respect for him rising almost to the point of admiration."

On the beach below were trypots, "and there we found a party of men busy extracting the oil from the heaps of blubber cut up from the huge humpback whale; flukes and wreck on the beach - - - . They were dripping and fairly saturated with oil, and everything around was in the same condition. The stinking fluid had run down the face of the bluff to the water's edge, and the whole place was redolent of the perfume. A row of casks filled with oil testified to the success of the business."

This picture was repeated farther north, at Pillar Point and Moss Beach, as well as at other promontories on the California coast. Significant also is the fact that in the 1860's Portuguese immigration had already begun, not only for whaling but here and there a Portuguese family had taken over a farm.

Traditional Chamarita Festival in the 1890's at Half Moon Bay. (Below) Alexander Moore home in Pescadero, built in 1853 and still in use.

Loren Coburn's hotel, "Coburn's Folly," at Pebble Beach, Pescadero's greatest asset as a resort town. (Below) Ocean Shore Railroad passengers continue their journey via Stanley Steamer at Tunitas.

Ocean Shore passengers view Coastside scenery.

## SANTA CRUZ

OCEAN SHORE — REACHES THE BEACHES

**THROUGH SERVICE**
VIA

## RAIL-AUTO and RAIL

### 30-MILE AUTOMOBILE TRIP

| SOUTH BOUND Read Down | | DAILY SCHEDULE | NORTH BOUND Read Up | |
|---|---|---|---|---|
| Leave | 8.10 A. M. | San Francisco | 12.40 P. M. | Arrive |
| Arrive | 10.15 " | Tunitas Glen | 10.45 A. M. | Leave |
| Leave | 10.30 " | Tunitas Glen | 10.15 " | Arrive |
| " | 10.45 " | San Gregorio | 9.45 " | Leave |
| " | 11.15 " | Pescadero | 9.15 " | " |
| " | 11.45 " | Pigeon Point | 8.45 " | " |
| " | 12.00 Noon | Gazos Creek | 8.30 " | " |
| " | 12.10 P. M. | Torquay | 8.20 " | " |
| " | 12.20 " | Waddell Creek | 8.10 " | " |
| Arrive | 1.00 " | Swanton | 7.50 " | " |
| Leave | 1.05 " | Swanton | 7.50 " | Arrive |
| Arrive | 1.55 " | Santa Cruz | 7.00 " | Leave |

A 5½ HOUR MOVING PICTURE RIDE. THE MOST
FASCINATING SCENERY IN CALIFORNIA. CLIFFS—
BLUFFS BEACHES ROCKS REDWOODS GARDENS
AND MARINE SCENERY.

- - DEPOT - -

**12th and Mission Street, San Francisco**

Make your reservations for Seat Space
on automobile in advance

For further information Phone Market 50

**"THE COOL SCENIC ROUTE"**

The Ocean Shore Railroad operated out of San Francisco and
Santa Cruz during the years 1907-
1920. Although construction was
never completed, the railroad provided Stanley Steamer stage service across the unfinished gap.

Farmers of the 1890's leaving their milk at the Pescadero Cheese Factory

Robert I. Knapp (left) was an enterprising manufacturer who built wagons and side-hill plows for Coastside farmers at his shop in Half Moon Bay.

(Below) School teachers of the Gay Nineties in Half Moon Bay: Rose Shubert, Meg Campbell, George Gilchrist, George Williams, and Mamie Quinlan.

Meantime Spanishtown, at the cross-roads entrance to the Coastside, was becoming a kind of miniature metropolis to the Coastside. Apparently it was not much to look at, for one traveler paused only to say it "contains little to attract a stranger", and another saw from the stagecoach "mostly whiskey and blacksmiths".

But it had in fact much more. George Borden and Rufus Hatch (father of Alvin but no relation to James) operated a sawmill in Purissima Canyon, and sold lumber in town. James Hatch's water-powered grist mill on Pilarcitos Creek saved for many Coastside inhabitants the cost of shipping grain out and flour in, while Robert I. Knapp, with tread-mill horse power on the site that later held the Ford garage, manufactured his own patented side-hill plow. He also built wagons and carriages, did general blacksmithing, and published a newspaper.

All this, plus a brewery, a hotel, and stores, gave to the Coastside a somewhat balanced economy. It also meant that Half Moon Bay, which was gradually dropping its nickname, Spanishtown, had become a sizeable village; in fact in 1892 its newspaper claimed for it a thousand inhabitants. Certain it is that the town was, for a period, Redwood City's only rival for the distinction of being the county's largest town, and the political boast was, "as goes Spanishtown so goes the county".

As for outside contacts, the stagecoach, Wells Fargo Express, and, from the late 1860's, the telegraph, kept the Coastside in touch with the Bayside, but its heaviest trade was by ship with San Francisco from the harbor at Pillar Point and in lesser amounts from other shipping points. Routine announcements in the *Coast Advocate* during the 1890's spoke of the steamer *Gypsy* that sailed every Friday from San Francisco with freight for Half Moon Bay. Another steamer was "due at Amesport Sunday, weather permitting", and the steamer *Santa Cruz* had carried off "6,000 sacks of grain on Saturday night and completed her cargo at Pigeon Point where she took aboard several hundred barrels of whale oil".

Between Half Moon Bay and Pescadero, in those days of horsedrawn communication, was a string of other incipient villages, each bearing the name of the creek on which it stood, and each boasting a "hotel", a bar, and a country store. Four miles from Half Moon Bay was Purissima which had also its cemetery and its school of 40 or 50 pupils, blacksmith shop, and the imposing home of Henry Dobbel. Next was Lobitos which in 1892 was hopefully called "headquarters for oil wells", and there was a tavern at Tunitas.

San Gregorio, in its broad and fertile valley, was called by the *Coast Advocate* a "small village" and its hotel a "popular resort" where sometimes people with nationally famous names stopped for hunting and fishing. Symbolizing the unity of the entire Coastside, was the firm of Levy Brothers which, beginning in Half Moon Bay in 1872, had established branches in San Gregorio and Pescadero, and had acquired ownership of the stagecoach line from San Mateo plus the Wells Fargo Express agency. At the turn of the century, the firm moved its headquarters to San Mateo.

While Coastside producers experimented with devices for ocean shipping, none of which was ever completely successful south of Pillar Point, they dreamed increasingly of a railroad. Surely the railroad age, the era when new crisscross bands of steel were everywhere binding the country closer together, would sooner or later bring rails to this productive corner of the West. The depression of the 1870's put a damper on the prospect, but the prosperous 1880's revived it. The engineering problems were not insurmountable but they were expensive for the amount of revenue in prospect.

Another delaying influence was the profound change in the Coastside population that was taking place: the region was having to assimilate a large influx of Portuguese settlers, coming direct from the Azores.

As early as 1878 Mrs. Rufus Hatch noted in her diary that these foreigners were putting on a strange celebration—it seemed to have some religious significance but what it was she could not imagine. Undoubtedly this was the first enactment here of Chamarita, a folk festival that has become an annual all-community affair, not only in Half Moon Bay and Pescadero but also in a number of other California towns.

The legendary origin of this fiesta is found on the island of Fayal in the Azores; there the traditional celebration of the Feast of Pentecost has, for many generations, centered in the belief that at a certain time, long ago, the Holy Spirit miraculously intervened when the island's people were facing starvation through a failure of their crops, and a strange ship arrived unexpectedly, loaded with food. The master of the ship, says the legend, not only fed the starving people but refused any pay for his generosity.

Hence the central point of the celebration to this day is a free lunch, served to all comers without question or obligation. The practice is kept alive by a "Brotherhood of the Holy Spirit" (*Irmandade do Espiritu Santo,* hence the "I.D.E.S. Hall") which raises the funds and directs the celebration. A large silver crown is taken to the church and blessed, then, with much pageantry, it is carried at the head of a long parade to the Chamarita Hall where it remains during the day of feasting and dancing.

The strength of the Portuguese element in the population is made evident by the wide participation each year in this parade—every civic, community, or business organization of consequence takes part, from the high school band to the Odd Fellows Lodge. It is in part, no doubt, a response to the eagerness with which the Portuguese, on their part, undertook to become Americans. By the early 1890's, 125 men of Portuguese birth who had settled in San Mateo County had taken out citizenship papers and become voters. Four-fifths of these lived on the Coastside, and the same proportion were listed as farmers or dairymen; only fifteen were common laborers.

Assimilation is shown also in the many inter-marriages, and here and there in the changing of names. It comes as a slight shock to a stranger to learn, for instance, that a young man named Miller is Portuguese. It was Milla, he readily explains; he didn't change it purposely—he just got tired correcting people who mispronounced it. And a teacher could not understand why one of her brightest pupils, a girl named Terry, always took the side of the Portuguese in petty feuds between the Portuguese and the Irish. The answer: the name was really, or used to be, Terra.

To assimilate the Portuguese was easier for the Coastside than it would have been for many other places because this melting pot had already fused the original Spanish families with the Anglo-American and Irish. And with these processes all well under way, it was ready, without even giving it a thought, to take on still another wave of newcomers, this one from sunny Italy.

After the turn of the century, railroad rumors finally began to materialize. In 1905 the Ocean Shore Railway Company was incorporated, with a plan to build from San Francisco down the coast to Santa Cruz. Building, in fact, was begun simultaneously at both extremities, the immediate objective at the south end being the cement plant at Swanton. The revenue from the business of hauling cement would help finance the building of the rest of the line.

But bad luck dogged the enterprise from the start. The great barrier at San Pedro Point and the Devil's Slide was just about surmounted, with a tunnel at the Point, when the earthquake of 1906 not only obliterated much of the grade but also carried expensive equipment into the sea. Grading was resumed, however, and by 1907 trains were running from San Francisco to Moss Beach, by 1908 to Half Moon Bay, and later as far as "Tunitas Glen".

At the other end, the company enjoyed, for a time, the profitable business of hauling cement into Santa Cruz, but this was too good to last. A mysterious rival called the Coastline Railway was incorporated and built a parallel line from Santa Cruz northward, and up the valley direct to the Swanton cement plant. On completion of the line the mystery was solved—the new line was "bought out" by the Southern Pacific Company, and the Ocean Shore line lost the cement business.

For want of capital, the long un-built gap between Tunitas and Swanton, or Davenport Landing, was never closed. Passenger service from San Francisco to Santa Cruz—"the cool scenic route"—was maintained, however, by carrying passengers between the two railheads in a Stanley Steamer automobile.

Meanwhile, at the north end there was a real estate boom and many new "towns" were created on the map; lots were sold to eager Sunday excursionists, even to gullible distant investors who were willing to buy, sight unseen. Actual villages were born at Edgemar, Salada and Brighton Beaches (later Sharp Park), Vallemar, Rockaway, Tobin (San Pedro Terrace), Montara, Moss Beach, Princeton, Granada, Miramar, and Arleta Park.

Passenger traffic over the road, with the advertising slogan "It reaches the beaches", plus freight hauling to and from the Coastside towns and farms, kept it in operation for a dozen years, but the company never got out of the financial doldrums. Receiverships and the opposition of committees for the bond holders dogged its attempted moves forward and, in the end, its death knell was rung by the very medium that the railroad itself was using between its two stubs of track—the automobile.

Cars and trucks on improved roads slowly cut into the business; profits diminished and deficits grew. Finally in 1920 a petition to abandon the service was filed with the State Railroad Commission. The employees, perhaps unwittingly, hastened the inevitable by going on strike with a demand for higher wages. As a result the trains on the Ocean Shore never ran again.

While the death of the railroad brought disappointment and decay to a number of communities, the coming of the motor car marked the beginning of a new era for the Coastside. As the railroad had put an end to its ocean shipping, so motor trucks and buses took over from the railroad—rolling over the hills with relative ease and bringing the best solution yet to the Coastside's perennial shipping problem. Finally, with the building of a highway past the Devil's Slide and Pedro Point, it seemed that a true gateway to the region was opened, but years of washouts and landslides showed that a satisfactory passage was yet to be found.

Bigger changes are coming, however, and still another era in which transportation will no longer be a problem. The barriers that have made this a region apart will be down, or at least rendered ineffectual. Already a freeway has reached the northern area where the City of Pacifica was born full-grown with twenty thousand inhabitants.

Inevitably this freeway will find a passage over, around, or under Montara (San Pedro) Mountain, and another great arterial will open an easy way across the Peninsula from San Mateo. Already Half Moon Bay has incorporated in preparation for the flood of urban settlers that these events will bring, and the new breakwater at Pillar Point will provide a center for a whole new set of seaside activities. With these changes the old Coastside with its Spanishtown quaintness will be gone, forever.

Air view of seventeen cities, San Francisco to Palo Alto.

# VIII. Proliferating Cities: *Why so many?*

*"Progress is not automatic; freedom is no guarantee of right choice. But the great adventure goes on, confused by man's frailty, redeemed by his basic decency."*                                    AUGUST HECKSCHER

They call it a San Francisco affair — that famous earthquake of April 18, 1906, but it did not confine its destruction within the city's limits. Down the Peninsula it left in ruins the Stanford University campus, the courthouse and schools in Redwood City, a church and business houses in San Mateo, besides which, almost everybody had a fallen chimney or at least badly cracked walls. These areas escaped San Francisco's fate only because there were fewer buildings to be destroyed, and the shaking was not followed by a devastating fire.

But there was a long-run consequence down the Peninsula—one of a different nature and quite unexpected. Despite a quick recovery in the city, with new buildings springing phoenix-like out of the ruins, so many of the homeless refugees decided to try living "in the country", since they had to start over again somewhere, that they came down the Peninsula like a small avalanche, pushing at least the northern portion of San Mateo County without warning into a new era—that of the suburban "bedroom town".

The Peninsula happened, in some respects, to be ready for this break. Anticipating more commuters because of future Peninsula growth-estimates, an electric railway had, by 1906, been running cars to San Mateo for three years, with the promise of an extended network of lines to other towns. At the time of the disaster, the Southern Pacific Company was just completing its short-cut "Tunnel Route" into San Francisco along the Bay shore. This prospect of rapid transit had brought subdivisions into being from San Mateo to South San Francisco but, up to this time, lots were selling very slowly.

The pitiful flood of homeless refugees that came streaming out of San Francisco —afoot, on horseback, and on everything that had wheels—opened for hungry Peninsula realtors a vast new market. They joined with other sympathetic Peninsulans in helping to set up refugee camps, and then worked them assiduously. For the relatively fortunate victims who, perhaps, had insurance checks in their wallets, there were attracitve locations, say, near the millionaire homes "in Burlingame", while for the destitute there were other places where a twenty-five foot lot could be had for as little as $150, payable in small monthly installments. And you could live in a tent on your lot while you built your house.

All this was quite new. Urban life as we know it now was then unknown down the Peninsula. Even Redwood City and San Mateo, the only corporate municipalities in San Mateo County, were still Victorian villages. Redwood City had prospered on lumber shipping and the business of county government, but the householders' yards were still enclosed behind fences with gates and turnstiles, because cows and horses belonging to the villagers had always fed on the grass along the streets.

The town of San Mateo still lived largely on services rendered to its surrounding estates of wealthy men, and these, in turn, had the effect of hemming it in and preventing expansion. These barriers were breaking down by the turn of the century, however, particularly on land released by the Howards. And for those times, Redwood City's 1,653 people, and San Mateo's 1,832, made them cities of no mean size.

A glance at the other towns as they were in 1906 finds Menlo Park, like San Mateo, still "the village" for surrounding estates of wealthy gentlemen, while Belmont was similarly supplying the people up in the canyon. San Carlos had a handsome railway station but only a dozen families. Burlingame could still be described as but little more than a railway station and a country club, Millbrae was the Mills Estate plus a country store and a few houses. San Bruno was a station that served a rural area, and Colma was a farming village.

But besides these older villages there were two new towns that demand special notice; each was the product of a set of special events, and both were growing fast. The pair were the industrial city of South San Francisco and the university town of Palo Alto. Stanford University and Palo Alto were just over the border in Santa Clara County, but both belonged, and still do, in fact if not in law, almost equally to San Mateo County.

When G. F. Swift came west in search of a site for a Pacific Coast meat packing center, he found exactly what he was looking for on the Lux farm, which has since become the city of South San Francisco. Charles Lux, of Miller and Lux, who bought it in 1853 from the original Buri Buri owners, had recently died (1887) and the land was on the market. Swift saw at once that not only was the site near San Francisco, with transportation available by both water and rail, but it was also situated where prevailing winds would carry the offensive fumes of the slaughter houses out over the Bay.

His plan was for all of the large meat packing firms to join in establishing a stockyard to serve the packing plants that they, severally, would build. These would be on Point San Bruno at the water's edge, and up-wind toward the west would be the town where the employees would live.

Agreements were made to implement this plan, and, in 1891, title to the land and the job of promoting a town were turned over to a subsidiary corporation, the South San Francisco Land and Improvement Company. But there was fierce opposition to this bold venture; the established butchers of San Francisco fought it with the heaviest pressures they could bring to bear, with the result that all but Swift himself withdrew from the project. He refused to be intimidated, however, and carried on alone. In 1892 he established the stockyard and the Western Meat Company. In later years, Armour & Co. came into the enterprise and, to this extent, at least, Swift's original dream was finally fulfilled.

Other industries also moved into South San Francisco: W. P. Fuller & Co.'s paint factory in 1898, then Steiner's Terra Cotta and Pottery Works, and Doak Sheet Steel Company, now a part of Bethlehem Steel. Industries from then on increased in number and variety. The residential section began on a small plat west of the present Bayshore Freeway. Under the able promotion of W. J. Martin, it grew large enough by 1908 to become a city of the sixth class with nearly two thousand inhabitants.

The Palo Alto story begins with Leland Stanford, who was ex-Governor and United States Senator for California when he and Mrs. Stanford suffered the tragedy of losing their only son and the sole heir to their huge fortune. The grief-stricken parents then decided to invest their all, as a memorial to their son, in a great new university. The site chosen for it was their Peninsula farm, "Palo Alto", and there it first opened its doors to students in the fall of 1891.

The university campus was thus placed roughly midway between the two small towns of Menlo Park and Mayfield, either of which might conceivably have been considered the university town, though Menlo Park was the station and village most used by the Stanfords. But Senator Stanford and his business partner, Timothy Hopkins of Menlo Park, were unhappy about the saloons in these two rough-and-tumble villages and felt there should be a university town with a more wholesome moral environment for the students. Hence they projected an entirely new town, closer to the campus, with covenants written into the property deeds forever prohibiting the sale of alcoholic beverages—and prohibition in this form persists in Palo Alto even down to the present day of 1963.

Plans for the new town were made simultaneously with those for the university and, by 1891, in time for the opening, a village called Palo Alto had begun to take form as University Avenue was cut through a grain field to connect it with the campus entrance. By the turn of the century, it had become officially a city and was growing by leaps and bounds.

This variegated string of towns and villages had appeared spontaneously, without legal permission or control of any kind. Planning commissions and building permits were as yet unheard of. What little advance preparation there was for the burst of new urban growth of 1906 was the work of railroad men and a few real estate promoters. Each town, like Topsy, "just growed", and when, in its awkward adolescence it faced the need of tax money for police, fire protection, or street work, its only recourse, except for special districts which later became popular, was either to annex itself to an existing municipality (which in those days was not often possible) or to incorporate as a city with its own taxing power.

The latter was the more exciting thing to do, and it happened here so often that it became the natural and expected event—a kind of blessed event that kept recurring

South San Francisco's first store, 1893

Belmont General Store, on Old County Road.

Early view of B Street in San Mateo.

A hose company, San Mateo Volunteer Fire Department.

as the Peninsula, again and again, gave birth to another city. Coming down to the present, this Mother-Peninsula, with her numerous progeny crowding each other for space in this small county, reminds us with each new toddling city of the famous "old woman who lived in a shoe - - - ". Does she have too many children?

One serious attempt was made before World War I to create a regional urban authority within which this growth, with provision for local home rule, could have an orderly development. At least this would have been the effect, though it was not the primary purpose of the plan. The idea was to consolidate the Bay Area in a Greater San Francisco, united in a borough system similar to that of Greater New York; and San Mateo County at that time indicated its willingness to go along with such a proposal.

To do this required an enabling act by the State Legislature, and when that body failed to act on the proposal, an initiative petition was circulated and a state constitutional amendment placed on the ballot (1912). But the city of Oakland, fearing to lose its identity, and hoping to develop its water front to out-do that of San Francisco, launched an angry and successful campaign to convince the voters over the state that San Francisco was trying to annex the other Bay cities against their will. When the voting came, only San Mateo and Marin counties joined with San Francisco in giving the plan ballot box approval. The rest of the state voted solidly against it.

So, new towns have kept on appearing, like prairie crocuses in the spring. Probably this pattern of competing cities is not unlike other suburban areas throughout the country, except that here the limited space between Bay and Ocean gives added point to the question: how can these things be? *Why* does this small county have seventeen independent, incorporated cities, with more of them certain to follow —in fact, with no end in sight to this process of Balkanizing the Peninsula?

Some of these new towns, of course, are not new at all. They are survivals from the old farming life in the team-and-wagon days, when shipping points on railroads everywhere (in good farming areas) were only five to eight miles apart; and in regions where there was no railroad, country stores sold food and drink to the farmers and took in trade their butter and eggs. When the farmers began to drive automobiles, many of these country centers withered and died, but railroad villages, if near a large metropolis, found themselves transformed into suburbs.

These towns were supposed to remain forever small—small and simple, like the New England villages with their "pure democracy". The commuters wanted it this way—otherwise, how could they maintain the illusion of living in the country?

But the in-the-country illusion in time had to break down. Urban life in our time, including the *sub*-urban, refuses to remain small and simple. As the suburban town grows, the older commuters still walk to the train but the late comers are too far out; they find themselves driving their cars to the station, and this takes them over streets that badly need improving, to cramped or non-existant parking spaces. To get the necessary tax money, the dilemma must sooner or later be faced; taxing districts can make do for a time, but inevitably comes the pressure to incorporate. When this is done, the horrified commuter finds himself trapped in a city again.

Now he has two; one city to live in and another to work in! Instead of being simplified, his situation has become more complex. He is more urban than ever.

This pressure to incorporate comes in various forms. There is probably a tangle of taxing districts that is getting too expensive. Then there is the urge to keep up with the Joneses in the next town, and even if this is resisted, in time it becomes a question of survival. Jonesville, incorporated and booming, threatens to annex portions of unincorporated Smithville, perhaps ultimately all of it. But Smithville has an identity of its own, a history and a civic pride that make the thought of non-existence intolerable, especially if it means becoming a part of that "terrible Jonesville".

So, "We must incorporate or lose our identity" becomes the slogan that carries the day. In some instances, in addition to identity as a town, a certain pattern of living is at stake. To illuminate the various phases of this process, no better example could be found anywhere than the story of our own cities of Burlingame, Hillsborough, and Millbrae.

The name, Burlingame, had been on the map ever since Anson Burlingame, President Lincoln's Minister to China, bought a piece of property here, hoping, perhaps, to come back and make it his home. But Mr. Burlingame died instead. A survey was made on the property for a town to be named after him, but nothing of the kind developed until 1893 when, instead of a town, some of San Francisco's wealthiest men organized the Burlingame Country Club.

As the club prospered, its members contrived with the Southern Pacific Company to build a Burlingame railway station, primarily for their use, midway between the old villages of San Mateo and Millbrae. The growth of a city around the station was *not* a part of the club's plan—a village, perhaps, yes; but not a booming suburban metropolis. They did not reckon, of course, with the San Francisco disaster of 1906.

When the flood of refugees came, Burlingame quickly outstripped all of its neighbors in the sale of lots and the building of homes. So definitely in the public mind was the name associated with millionaires that to have a Burlingame address meant prestige, and property values there were notably higher than in neighboring towns.

Since this new Burlingame community lay contiguous to San Mateo, there were hopes among San Mateans that they might annex the area. But among the Burlingame people this idea never got so much as a hearing. They were not about to sacrifice the prestige that their name enjoyed by becoming a part of something else, least of all "an old town like San Mateo".

Burlingame shattered the precedents of those days for rapid growth. By 1908, when the people voted to incorporate, there were perhaps a thousand inhabitants; in 1910 there were 1,585, and by 1914 a special census showed 2,849.

Part of this lattermost leap in numbers was due to the annexation of the Broadway area which, up to that time, was known as the town of Easton. Ansel Mills Easton, whose father, Ansel I., had bought this property in 1860, was subdividing and selling off the land. As a part of his sales-promotion program, he provided a battery-driven street car that ran up Hillside Drive to bring his commuting customers down to the Easton station, now Burlingame-Broadway. In this new community there were no old settlers with a sense of a historic identity to preserve, hence the people there were easily persuaded to cast in their lot with Burlingame.

This expansion, and the burgeoning strength of Burlingame as a city, were a surprise and a threat to the members of the Burlingame Country Club. Theirs was, in truth, a *country* club, whose chief purpose was to provide a place to relax in rural surroundings. This new city of Burlingame was coming too close for comfort to their richly appointed homes and their exclusive golf course. The prospect of being taxed, regulated, and required to put in streets and sidewalks by a city in which they would be a minority of the voters although owners of a major part of the taxable wealth, was not what they had planned for.

They sought legal advice and were persuaded by their own Arthur H. Redington that their only sure defense was to incorporate a city of their own, in which they, and people of similar interests, would be a controlling majority. Thus was born the city of Hillsborough—a "city" whose main reason for existence was to maintain a rigorously "non-city" atmosphere.

The planners of the new city took care to include plenty of territory, covering most of the western borders at that time of Burlingame and San Mateo, and extending to the Spring Valley Water Company's property at the top of the hill; and when the town was organized it proceeded to set up lot-size regulations and building restrictions designed to discourage all but people of more than ordinary means. All city-like fittings such as sidewalks and checker-board streets were banned, and there was to be no business or commercial enterprise of any kind in the town.

Burlingame was now very nearly fenced in, with Hillsborough on the west and the D. O. Mills estate, which still remained intact, on the north. Until such time as the Mills property might go on the market, there remained only one small opening through which Burlingame might expand, which it later did, northwestward to the Skyline Boulevard.

Millbrae's dilemma, on the other hand, was long drawn-out and controversial, because there the people faced two clear-cut alternatives: to annex to Burlingame and lose their identity as Millbrae, or to incorporate and remain forever a small city.

For many years Millbrae was only a small satellite of the Mills estate, from which it got its name and its railway station. Some growth was brought by the Porcelain Works (1919), which is now the Container Factory, but real suburban growth came only in the 1920's when the firm of Niels Schultz & Gus Miller & Sons opened a new Millbrae Highlands subdivision with attractive homes. And Niels Schultz was no absentee developer. He lived in his own tract and made himself and his family a friendly part of the community they were building. This is an important part of the story, for Schultz did his clever best to put off the day of decision—to keep the people who were buying his houses from trying to decide, then and there, the future of their community.

His chief difficulty was with those who looked favorably in the direction of Burlingame. Not only did the name still radiate the glamor of its original association with the Country Club, but the town itself was known as a stylish and progressive city. The Millbrae name on the other hand, though old, did not carry great weight at first, for most of the inhabitants were newcomers who had not yet acquired an appreciation of its historical background.

Between Millbrae and Burlingame lay the Mills Estate with a thousand or more choice, undeveloped acres, even after a portion of it had been annexed to Burlingame as Ray Park and Burlingame Village. If the two should become one city, this vacant land would be a great asset rather than a problem, and there would be room, by housing standards then in vogue, for the enlarged Burlingame to become a city of at least 60,000 inhabitants. If not, there would be two towns of half the size, and the land lying between them would almost certainly become a bone of bitter contention.

Discussion of Millbrae's future began early. In February, 1929, a group called the Millbrae Development Association invited the Burlingame Chamber of Commerce and city officials to present whatever inducements they could offer in favor of annexation to Burlingame.

The list looked impressive. Extended to Millbrae almost immediately would be fire protection and lower insurance rates; house-to-house mail delivery; street lights; sewers; better schools; and easier loans for building purposes. The cost in taxes, it was estimated, would be only 43 cents per hundred dollars of assessed value above their present county tax. However, no definite action followed the discussions.

The first political showdown came almost two years later, on January 30, 1931, when, as a result of a petition signed by well over 150 residents, the question of annexation to Burlingame was decided in an official election. The expectation was, almost up to election day, that annexation would win. But the tally of votes turned out to be only 68 for annexation and 230 against. As one newspaper analyst pointed out, more than a hundred people who had petitioned for a chance to vote on annexation changed their minds and voted against it. What had happened?

Some say that the Burlingame officials and Chamber-of-Commerce men overplayed their hand and aroused suspicion by seeming too anxious. But there were also said to be "powerful interests" working against annexation—a term that was understood to mean the Mills Estate owners and the Schultz organization. If annexation took place it would include the Mills acreage, or at least most of it, thereby making it subject to city taxation. In fact, one of the points emphasized by the Burlingame "advisers" was that, because of certain provisions in the law, by annexing promptly, this acreage could be easily included as a large taxable asset, whereas if Millbrae should later wish to incorporate separately, this could not be done without the consent of the owners.

Nobody knows the full story about pressures brought to bear, but for one thing, it was announced that if annexation were turned down and if Millbrae would, instead, organize its own fire district, there would be a cash donation of $3,000 available for the purchase of fire-fighting equipment.

Meantime, Niels Schultz set up an information service for the people of Millbrae, his friends and neighbors. Four consecutive bulletins were prepared and delivered house-to-house in Millbrae, counseling against annexation. The last of the bulletins

These portals of the past, colorful gates erected by Messrs. Oliver and McGlynn, gave Menlo Park its name.

(Below) Camp Fremont Hospital Unit at Menlo Park during World War I.

View of Pedro Valley, now in the City of Pacifica.

Salada Beach, now the business district of Pacifica.

appeared the night before the election, urging that this weighty question about Millbrae's future should have more study, and ending with the punch line, "You can always get into Burlingame, but once you are in, you can never get out".

Old-time Millbrae patriots like to tell another story about that pre-election night —a story of how Schultz headed off a pro-Burlingame rally. The Burlingame *Advance* had announced a meeting in the school house, called by the Millbrae Protective Association, at which county officials and Burlingame people would be present to answer questions. But Schultz asked first for the school house key, so the story goes, kept it in his pocket, and explained in his famous fourth bulletin that the newspapers were mistaken and there would be no meeting.

So the only people who showed up for the meeting were the delegation from Burlingame and a few pro-Burlingame stalwarts in Millbrae. They all waited outside. It appeared, on enquiry, that everybody in town who had a school house key was away from home that night, so the waiting went on while someone drove to the Principal's house in Burlingame for a key. Finally it came, and the zealous waiters all went inside to tell each other there what a fine town Burlingame was!

Following these events, fifteen years went by, carrying with them a Great Depression and a World War, before Millbrae actually came to the point of deciding its own future. During this time, as the town grew, the necessary services were obtained by a pyramid of special taxing districts: three of them for water; three for street lights; and one each for sewer, fire protection and police; plus one for public utilities in general.

The idea of annexation to Burlingame did not die, but it became a minority opinion, as the Millbrae "identity" idea gained strength. However, nobody knew how strong this identity feeling was and a succession of committees, associations and leagues kept the matter alive. In 1944 a Taxpayers' Committee published a long and detailed analysis of the pros and cons of annexation *vs.* incorporation. But the leanings of the committee were betrayed by its statement that "the first thing to contemplate" on the annexation side "is the loss of our identity". Its true feelings were further shown by its assurance that the Burlingame tax would be at least $1.00 per $100.00 of assessed value, whereas Millbrae alone, by careful management, might get by on thirty-five cents. The committee did not venture to predict how long the city might exist on so small a tax.

One curious fact, here and in other such situations, was the absence of any attempt to answer the basic question: how large does a city *need* to be to give its people, not only the bare necessities of government, but also such needful things as a public library and recreational facilities?

Finally, in 1946, the people of Millbrae took the plunge of petitioning for a yes-or-no vote on incorporation, and the result (December 11) was 1,038 to 278 in favor of becoming the county's thirteenth city.

There ensued a long legal contest with Burlingame over the Mills Estate property, which the Millbrae people assumed was theirs by right of history, but Burlingame refused to recognize any such right. For more than a year, the two communities fought each other, step by step, through the courts, albeit with a notable lack of bitterness, even though, during that time, a court injunction at Burlingame's request prohibited Millbrae's elected officials from assuming the duties of their offices.

The quarrel was finally settled by an out-of-court division of the territory. From January 6, 1948, Millbrae functioned as a bona fide city, and in January, 1954, all suits still pending were cancelled.

"I will help you all I can with the history of Colma, but I am *not interested in Daly City!*" These words, spat vehemently from the lips of an old-time resident of Colma, voiced the deep feelings of people in a historic town that, merely by doing nothing, actually lost its identity. They will also serve to introduce a new and vigorous city that sprang into being as a direct result of the San Francisco earthquake and fire.

When this disaster struck, John Daly's milk ranch was operating on Daly's Hill, just outside the San Francisco city limits. Across the way still stood the old Abbey House, and southward were the village of Colma, fields of vegetables, and hog ranches. On forgotten maps of some of the territory near Daly's Hill there were streets and lots, but these represented, for the most part, only forlorn hopes of past years.

But the old maps quickly came alive, and new ones appeared, when the San Francisco refugees began to think of a new and permanent place to settle. Temporary shelters provided for them in Golden Gate Park and other open spaces were ordered cleared away before the winter of 1907-08; refugee families were given the privilege of buying their standardized, temporary homes for twenty dollars each, and for another twenty a man could have his home hauled—family and all—to a site of his choosing.

Daly's Hill being within easy hauling distance, and lots there being obtainable on easy terms, the pasture and open spaces became lots again and soon were filled with these temporary shelters, some of which became permanent parts of new homes. Grocery stores appeared also in temporary buildings, a barber shop in a tent, enterprising men piped in water, and thus, suddenly a town appeared.

Although the settlement, for a while, looked like just another refugee camp, these people had bought property and had come to stay. Hence, they very soon had to face up to the matter of grading their hillside streets, controlling their water supply, and coping with all the similar problems of trying to live decently. In 1911 they voted to incorporate and chose to name their town Daly City after the benevolent, white-haired gentleman who had welcomed them to his milk ranch and through all their difficulties had been a kind and generous neighbor. Next came the voting of $100,000 in bonds for a municipal water system, then the building of a city hall, and by 1920 the new city's population was rapidly approaching four thousand.

This swift expansion was spreading in all directions from the hill top, especially down the southward slope toward the ancient fork in the road where, ever since mission days, travelers had taken either the right hand trail for San Pedro Valley, or the left one for San Mateo. At this point stood the village of Colma, then fifty years old as an American farming center. In this neighborhood still lived some of the descendants of the settlers who, in 1853, bought their land, but later found themselves evicted and forced to fight a long legal battle with the claimants of Rancho Lake Merced.

Now the Colma villagers, feeling secure in their history, ignored the warnings that, if they wished to preserve their name and identity, they had better make their existence legal. They stood their ground, as they thought, only to see the ground annexed, an insignificant bit at a time, by Daly City. Finally, they were all in Daly City, with nothing left of their old Colma but the name, the post office, and the no-longer-used railway station.

But, curiously enough, the Colma story does not end here. Colma as a historic village was gone forever but by an unpredictable chain of events, the name was rescued and given a new identity.

Bordering Colma on the southeast there had appeared a community of cemeteries, forced for lack of space to move out of San Francisco. Beginning with Holy Cross (1887), by 1904 there were ten cemeteries in the immediate area, the result of a San Francisco ordinance that prohibited burials in the city after August 1, 1901.

As years passed and population increased, the cemetery owners worried over their new status. Might the time not come when again they would be forced to move? After a long study of ways to protect themselves, directed mainly by Mattrup Jensen of Olivet Memorial Park, they came to the only possible conclusion: they must incorporate a town that the cemetery interests could control.

Acting on this conclusion, in 1924 they marked out an area that contained the necessary number of living inhabitants (500) and laid their problem before these people, asking for their cooperation. The people responded well and the town was organized. They were told that after the incorporation was consummated they could vote themselves out of the town if they wished. But when the citizens found themselves enjoying the benefits of being in a city with virtually no cost to them because the cemeteries carried the tax load, almost nobody wanted out.

All the problems, it seemed now, were solved, except one that was not foreseen—the matter of the town's name. On filing papers of incorporation, the chosen name, Memorial Park, was rejected by the County Supervisors because the county's new recreation center was already named Memorial Park. So a hasty choice was made and the town was christened Lawndale. But when this was finished and legally sanctioned, another difficulty arose: the city could never have its own post office, for California already had a Lawndale Post Office.

It took a little time to find an answer to this one. But, ultimately, the curious fact was brought out that while nascent Lawndale was a town without a post office, right next door was old Colma which had become a post office without a town. The simple action then was to hold an election in which the people of brief-lived Lawndale voted to change the name of their town to Colma. This done, the people of the cemetery city, the dead as well as the living, could rest peacefully without fear of having to move.

The town of Colma is outwardly governed by the usual elected officials, who are generally either cemetery employees or are engaged in related business such as monuments or flowers But the real policy-making is done by an unofficial body, a kind of luncheon club whose members are managers, owners, or representatives of the various cemeteries. In this way the affairs that are the common concern of these heterogeneous groups who own cemeteries—religious, racial, national, and people in business for a profit—are made to move along smoothly.

One more city of the San Mateo Peninsula, San Bruno, owes its start in life to the San Francisco disaster of 1906. Its name is among the oldest on the Peninsula, for the San Bruno Mountains had been on the map since the earliest Spanish beginnings. The San Bruno toll road of the 1860's that reached into San Francisco via the Bay shore, together with Richard Cunningham's San Bruno House at the railway crossing, brought the name down to the flats. But until 1906, San Bruno meant little more than a railway station and a post office.

Then came the two streams of stricken refugees out of the burning city, down the only two then-existing roads of escape, which converged at San Bruno. (They later became at that point El Camino Real and San Mateo Avenue.) Between these two roads a refugee camp was set up, offering temporary shelter and free food.

Soon these homeless people were visited by enterprising real estate salesmen with tempting offers of an opportunity to live "in the country". There was rapid transit to San Francisco via either steam train or electric cars, also jobs in near-by South San Francisco. A huge sign on the side of a barn announced "Lots for $225 and up, payable at $5.00 monthly". Thus San Bruno caught the first impact of fleeing refugees, and it quickly mushroomed into a suburban town.

But with the first winter rains the people of the new San Bruno began to realize they had problems, just the opposite in nature to those in Daly City. The two main roads, mentioned above, were graded and surfaced, and in 1912, signaling the opening era of the automobile, a ceremony at San Bruno marked the beginning in California of state-financed road work on El Camino Real. But the streets in the adjoining subdivisions each winter became impassable quagmires of mud. There was only one way to solve this problem, and in 1914 a large majority voted to incorporate. The election was followed by a gala celebration with a King (Harry Cook) and a Queen (Edith Schmidt) on horseback in a long parade, with speeches, music, and much enthusiasm. The whole affair was so successful that the King and Queen decided to play it for keeps and got married.

The growth of cities down the Peninsula has been rapid, but it has not moved as a continuously flowing stream, but rather by spurts and episodes, resembling, in a striking way, the quantum theory of expansion in the Universe. The wave of expansion following the earthquake of 1906 was ended by the nation's entering World War I. After the war, the booming 1920's saw another "quantum" of growth, but this was followed by the Great Depression and World War II. Now (1963) San Mateo County is in the midst of another period of expansion, the most unpredictable of all and, one might say, of almost incalculable magnitude.

The years of the "Roaring" 1920's brought to the County an over-all increase that more than doubled the population. The Roaring Decade also added to the incorporated list four new cities. But only one of these, San Carlos, was wholly new; the other three, Belmont, Menlo Park, and Atherton, were already communities of long standing.

Menlo Park and Atherton, the latter known then as Fair Oaks, had talked incorporation before. The Fair Oaks people, like those of Hillsborough, who had just incorporated for defense against the encroachment of burgeoning Burlingame, were prepared to resist Menlo Park's ambition to include their properties within its boundaries. But the matter was settled at that time in a unique, neighborly agreement.

On September 10, 1911, there was a meeting of committees appointed by the electors of Menlo Park and Fair Oaks at which a line was carefully drawn on a map to be taken as the boundary between the two towns "in the pending proceedings for incorporation", or in "any proceedings hereafter to be instituted by either town". The map was signed for Menlo Park by A. G. C. Hahn, John B. Kelly, Harry B. Morey, Sr., and John McBain; and for Fair Oaks by George A. Batchelder, Perry Eyre, George M. Wilcox, W. L. Growall, Clarence R. Walter, and Thomas H. Breeze.

But the proceedings then pending were not carried through, and the interesting map has now become a museum piece but nothing more. Twelve years and a World War intervened to overshadow such things, with Camp Fremont, a huge army training center complete with artillery range, at Menlo Park; after all this the boundary agreement was conveniently forgotten.

In 1923, proposals were once more up for discussion in Menlo Park, apparently with the hope again of including some of the valuable Fair Oaks-Atherton property. This time, at a meeting on the subject, with both communities represented, somebody lost his self-restraint, hot words were bandied about, and the Fair Oaks men bolted the meeting. The affair then became a race to be first in filing incorporation papers at the County Seat, and Fair Oaks came in just one hour and twenty minutes ahead of Menlo Park. But the new town was officially named Atherton instead of Fair Oaks because the latter name was found to have been pre-empted by a town in Sacramento County. The boundary line that now became legal was not far from the one previously agreed upon but more crooked and complex, and less to the liking of Menlo Park.

The people of Menlo Park, frustrated in their "imperialistic" ambitions, put off incorporation until 1927. But the matter could not be evaded indefinitely, especially when large numbers of new settlers moved in, forcing the town out of its old village-for-estates category and making it mainly a town for commuters and for Stanford University folk. Menlo Park has since annexed large areas to the east and the west, affording the city plenty of room for further expansion.

San Carlos, a really "new" town, blossomed out for the first time in the 1920's, after three abortive attempts to create a living community on the historic T. G. Phelps Dairy farm. Promoters of the earliest attempt (1887) built a beautiful railway station but succeeded in getting only a dozen families to move in. The second syndicate spent huge sums of money to create an illusion of big success (1907) but ended in bankruptcy. Only after World War I did it appear that the time for a town was ripe. Perhaps it was the timely, friendly genius of Fred Drake that brought success.

So rapidly did population increase that, by 1925, the town was not only ready for incorporation, but was on its way to win fame as the West's fastest growing town. Even in the Depression decade of the 1930's, its population more than trebled.

The early stages of this growth, and particularly the threat of spreading north-ward, frightened Belmont into action, to avoid what was then happening to old Colma. A town with such memories as the Angelo House, the Ralston mansion, and the temporary county seat, could not think of letting itself be absorbed by an upstart neighbor. Its incorporation, after being delayed by a law suit with San Carlos over the boundary, took effect in 1927. It remained small for some time but in recent years, with industries and new residential sections, Belmont has become one of the liveliest cities on the Peninsula.

The decade of the 1950's brought to San Mateo County an unbelievable flood of new people (more than 20,000 a year) and four entirely new cities. But the cities were formed, it would seem, more in reaction to this in-rush of settlers than either by or for them. First to move for incorporation was Woodside, and the instigating threat there was not the usual one of encroachment by other cities, though Atherton and Redwood City were remotely feared, but the appearance of subdividers in Woodside.

What with farms and the estates of monied men, land in the Woodside-Searsville valley was still held in sizeable acreages. When some of these holdings were sold and cut up into lots, even though the operation was carried out under the control of the County Planning Commission, and the homes erected were not cheap in any sense, the prospect raised by these changes was not pleasing to the older inhabitants. They foresaw the gradual devastation of the wooded countryside and the spawning in its place of blatant rows of streets and houses.

There was an urgent demand for home rule that could put restrictions on such development. Most of the people were not sure just what restrictions should be imposed, but on one thing there was wide agreement: the decision should be made *in* Woodside, and the reins of control should be held *in* Woodside.

After the usual arguments and false starts, the vote was taken on October 20, 1956, and Woodside became another city which was formed to keep itself from really becoming a city. Enough countryside was included to make it at least a rural kind of city—an irregular twelve square miles extending from Palm Circle on Cañada Road southward past Searsville Lake, eastward at one point to the Alameda de las Pulgas, and westward in two prongs reaching up the mountain side, one as far as Skyline Boulevard. The area now constitutes a city, but one with a density of less than three hundred inhabitants per square mile.

The new city officials began by zoning the area for residence lots of from one to three acres, depending upon topography. On the steep mountain side even larger tracts are required, varying in size as the terrain may permit. Removal of existing vegetation was prohibited except under specific regulations, and particular care was enjoined to prevent erosion. Existing commercial areas were zoned as such, with the obvious intent to keep them at a minimum.

The city of Pacifica came into being in a manner surprising to everyone. This was not an existing town fearful of losing its identity—it actually included a chain of small coastside communities which did lose their identity, and it emerged, at a single stroke, a full-grown city of twenty thousand souls.

What compelling circumstances brought this about? First, the usual things: the sudden growth of new subdivisions, a tangle of expensive taxing districts, and the immediate need of new facilities. But these might easily have produced not one but two, or even three cities separated from each other by both distance and hills. On the north, dating from the Ocean Shore Railroad days, were Laguna Salada and Brighton Beach which had united to become Sharp Park, plus Edgemar which had been all but swallowed up by the brand new community of Pacific Manor.

At the south end of the area was the old village of Pedro Valley or San Pedro Terrace, now lost in a wholly new community of Linda Mar, while between these two extremes, in a separate valley, lay Rockaway Beach and Vallemar. Anyone glancing at this geography, and at the history of previous developments on this Peninsula, might well have predicted two cities, one on each end, with the two quarreling over the middle. Fortunately, instead of any such traditional thing, a sense of unity in the whole area prevailed.

Today's earth-moving equipment has triumphed over hills of ordinary size, and this fact has helped to bring the local communities together. At the same time, the larger hills—the Peninsula's central ridge on the east and San Pedro Mountain on the south—have given to the people of the north-coast region a feeling of isolation from the rest of the County. They are much more directly attached, in their daily travel and communications, with San Francisco, yet are without a sense of belonging in either direction. This aloneness no doubt also helped in Pacifica; it gave the people a sense of a common woe, hence a reason for getting together.

Probably the culminating push was the attempted annexation by San Bruno of a strip reaching through the heart of this coastal area to the sea, which was defeated only by a political revolt in San Bruno itself. This threat from the outside helped strongly to win votes for incorporation without further delay. On October 29, 1957, the election was held, resulting in 2,601 "yes" votes and 2,113 "noes". But, despite this narrow margin of victory at the start, the city of Pacifica has since developed a strong community spirit.

The County's oldest town, Half Moon Bay, became in 1959 its newest organized city—just 113 years after the first settlers came to the little village of San Benito. Sitting alone on the Coastside, from time immemorial, the town had had its advocates of incorporation but the conservative property owners were able to keep them quiet. What was it that finally brought about the taking of the big step?

Curiously, there was no immediate threat to the community, nor any circumstances, new and pressing, to force the issue. But there was an old grievance, mild but long-felt, which at last was fanned into flame. It was the ancient complaint, in countless places, against absentee government—in short, a demand for home rule.

Some old-timers recalled the "good old days" when the county supervisors were elected by districts and each individual supervisor was the boss in his own little empire, arranging at his own discretion road improvements and patronage favors of many kinds for his constituents. The system might not be the best kind of county government, they said, but at least they knew whom they were dealing with; he lived right there and he had the final say-so.

In those times, too, there was a local constable and justice of the peace, instead of a big centralized sheriff's office and the courts away off over the hill. And another "nuisance" of modern times was the Planning Commission. Planning there must be, the argument ran, but conditions on the Coastside did not yet fit into the rules which were made, in fact, for towns on the Bay side but which were enforced everywhere.

The man who nursed these complaints for a purpose, working long and patiently like a skilled demagogue, was John L. "Nick" Carter. But nobody thought of calling Nick a demagogue, and his ultimate purpose, as people in time came to see it, could hardly be called anything less than constructive. In his mind was a dream of an incorporated Coastside, or as much of it as possible—a natural geographical region with a unity and a voice of its own.

Against the short-sighted opposition of tax payers, he mobilized the equal pettiness of complainers to win support for the basic first step—that of creating a legalized city of Half Moon Bay. No matter if its area was small to start with; time and more patient endeavor could take care of that. With the city officially established, he, and those who shared his dream, instead of nursing complaints could talk community pride. This, they hoped, would then be a commodity no longer in short supply. In this, as it turned out, their hopes have been realized.

Not that the previous arguments were all negative or entirely based on protest. Everyone could see changes that forced them to think of the future: the building of the breakwater; the developers eagerly buying up land; the community enthusiasm in the new city of Pacifica to the north of them. The incorporation proposal, timed in step with these events, could not help but make sense.

The election was held June 23, 1959; the result was 362 to 146, and on July 15, at 3:05 P. M., notice was received by telephone from Sacramento that the papers were filed, and Half Moon Bay became a self-governing city with the Honorable John L. Carter as its first mayor.

There had been, as always, arguments and negotiations over territory to be included within the city limits, but finally agreed upon was a strip along the coast, averaging about a mile in width, from Miramar southward to Cañada Verde—a total of five square miles. The population within this area is admittedly small but everybody knows that shortly will come the day when quaint old Half Moon Bay will be submerged in a sea of new and modern housing.

The process of city making goes on. With the closing of the year 1961, the seventeenth new city, Brisbane, slipped under the wire. Brisbane, as a town, was born in the times of the Great Depression. There had been a subdivision in 1908, at least on paper—an attempt to attract refugees of the earthquake and fire. Hillside lots without graded streets or utilities were offered for a mere thousand dollars each in a tract called Visitacion City, though it was a considerable distance removed from Visitacion Valley. Not many people seemed interested.

But twenty-odd years later, when the stock market crash left many city dwellers destitute, the situation became quite the reverse. Lots then were sold for as little as forty dollars, on terms of a dollar down and a dollar a week. Small bank loans for building were obtainable, and when the Federal Housing Administration plan of Federally-insured loans became operative, the hillside became covered with modest homes. By 1933 there were some four hundred of them.

The name, Brisbane, was introduced at this time by Arthur Ennis, the new agent for the tract; he said it was in honor of Arthur Brisbane, the popular columnist of that time for the Hearst newspapers. However, Ennis was a native of Brisbane, Australia, and he may well have been influenced also by memories of his boyhood.

The Brisbane people, in their steep hillside position, have long been troubled by the need for expensive street improvements, and at the same time by high taxes paid to overlapping utility districts. Annexation to South San Francisco was discussed, but the proposal did not seem attractive to either community. The belated planning of an industrial park on the floor of Guadalupe Valley, however, gave promise of a much needed source of tax revenue, and a way out of the dilemma. Fearing that South San Francisco might attempt to annex this prized portion of their area, the Brisbane people decided to forestall any such move by incorporating, and by undertaking from that point on to solve their own problems. Proceedings were consummated, and the city of Brisbane was officially born on November 24, 1961.

As the Peninsular cities have increased in number, community planning (along with assembly-line construction) has played an ever-more-important role in their development; but none of them has ever been as completely built according to plan as the now-proposed Foster City. Our earliest cities began with scarcely even a guess as to their ultimate size or the nature of what they might turn out to be, but Foster City, though as yet non-existent, is all planned in advance. Not one building has been erected (as of January, 1963), but complete specifications are on the drawing boards—not mere estimates, but listed items—almost as final and mandatory as are the blueprints for a house.

There will be a population of 35,000; they will live in 5,000 single-family homes, 1,600 town houses, and 4,400 apartment units. To serve these people, there will be nine elementary schools, two junior high schools, and one senior high school; there will be thirteen churches, 230 acres of parks and lagoons for recreation purposes, and 460 acres of industrial and commercial area which will provide an estimated 7,000 to 10,000 jobs and, of course, help with the taxes.

There is a popular impression that this "city of the future" is already a corporate municipality, but the more exact truth is this: not a city, but the Estero Municipal Improvement District was created in 1960 by special act of the State Legislature, with powers to tax, issue bonds, and to perform various other governmental functions. Bonds issued by this District provide the funds for development, and the bonded debt will be retired by taxes on the property after the community comes into being. The people may then either incorporate as a city, or annex themselves to another city, presumably San Mateo.

Besides planning the complete town before starting to build, the developers, T. Jack Foster & Sons, have also gone at their engineering problems in reverse. The site of Foster City is a flat area of some 2,600 acres approximately at sea level, known as Brewer Island. Reclaimed long ago from the marsh by the construction of levees, it has been farmed successfully for some fifty years; but for use as a city, the level must be raised and additional drainage provided. To accomplish this, instead of doing the usual thing—pulling down the hills to build up the flats—the Fosters are taking their fill from the bottom of the Bay.

On the shallow water over San Bruno Shoals, a giant dredge with two suction tubes is operating. The first tube picks up the layer of mud that covers a bed of sand, carries it back, and dumps it at the stern of the dredge, while the other tube, mounted amidships, brings up pure sand which it deposits in a barge. The loaded barge, equipped with bottom gates, is then pushed to a drydock at Foster City, where with the pressing of a button it dumps its cargo, and the sand is then pumped through pipes to the desired places. Top soil from the island itself will cover this sand when the desired level has been attained.

When completed, the entire area of Foster City will be slightly bowl-shaped, with drainage into a lake some four miles long that will wind through the center of the city. This lake will also provide boating (by sail and paddle only) for the dwellers. The level of the lake will be controlled by pumps and tide gates and will vary not more than two feet, but planners and engineers are sure it will be adequate to take care of the run-off from any rains that may occur.

Where the city-making seeds will sprout next is anybody's guess. There are whispers that it might be at La Honda, deep in the San Gregorio Valley, a resort, as well as a lumbering-and-ranching center since the 1870's. Or might it be among the crowding cottages on King's Mountain? Or in Ravenswood? Or Pescadero? It could even happen in some so-far-unsuspected spot—one that is now open pasture land.

A few people have wondered out loud whether the seemingly-endless pro-liferating of cities on the Peninsula is good or bad. In the American tradition of freedom there is much to be said in favor of local home rule and of self-determination for small communities. If the people of a given community want to maintain a small city, even though it costs them more than to join with another, who would wish to deny them the privilege? And the matter of cost is not altogether conclusive; whether a hundred thousand people in one city can actually govern themselves less expensively than if they were divided into a dozen cities is not as clear-cut or certain as it might be.

But students of urban problems have more than once pointed out that this Balkanizing process suggests the need for a new kind of regional government. Caspar W. Weinberger, as quoted in the public press, put it this way:

"We do not know whether the era of individual cities is closing, but we do know that the era of metropolitan areas is well upon us. In the San Francisco Bay Area we have 3 ½ million people and more than 600 special governmental units. If we are ever to see a reduction in governmental costs and taxes, we will have to have some kind of overall organization, fully responsible to the people, that has both the power and the skill to seek area-wide solutions to these area-wide problems."

Even more to the point, just as this book goes to the printer, comes a report in the public press that Governor Edmund G. Brown will ask the State Legislature to create a "local agencies formation commission". This commission, says the Gover-nor, would establish a regime of "planned parenthood for cities". He too must have been thinking about the old woman who lived in a shoe!

San Mateo County Courthouse, after the Great Earthquake of 1906.

Stanford University, following the quake.

Jennings' Livery Stable, San Mateo, April 18, 1906.

(Below) Many of San Francisco's standardized refugee cottages, set up in Golden Gate Park, were moved to Daly's Hill in 1907. These three, remodeled, became permanent Daly City homes.

San Francisco's Crystal Springs Dam, in San Mateo County, supplies
water both for the City and for the Peninsula suburbs.

# IX. Good Neighbors: *or are we?*

*"One craves to see great themes sought and discussed, great causes espoused. One burns for the re-introduction into life of the pursuit of greatness."*
CHARLES H. MALIK

The illusive, imaginary line that forms San Francisco's southern boundary is a most remarkable divider. Written into the statutes in 1856, it runs invisibly through back yards and bedrooms and is in some places difficult to find even for taxing purposes, yet it has so far proved to be an unbreakable barrier to that city's ambitions to expand. It is, in fact, two lines—a county boundary and the city limits.

Cities usually find it easy to expand within a county by annexing contiguous bits of territory. Supposedly the same could be done across a county line but the business of governing a city in two counties involves so many complications that it is generally considered impossible, or at least not worth the trouble.

Hence, for a city shut in as San Francisco is, the only practicable way to expand is to begin by moving or eliminating the county line, which requires an act of the State Legislature—and in this case an amendment to the State Constitution. All this, of course, is not impossible to bring about, or so it would seem, but experience has shown that the whole maneuver can become tremendously complicated.

San Francisco's first major move in this direction was not a mere moving of a county line but the attempt to create a Greater San Francisco covering the entire Bay Area, after the example set by Greater New York. It was undertaken at a seemingly auspicious time (1912). Despite the scandals of the late Schmitz-Reuf regime, the popular image of San Francisco generally was still good. The city's historic rebuilding of itself so completely atop the ruins of 1906 had caught the popular imagination, and its preparations to invite the whole world in 1915 to the Panama Pacific International Exposition further enhanced its prestige.

But the Greater San Francisco plan, which contemplated a system of self-governing boroughs, died before it was born. Even the preparatory step of amending the State Constitution was defeated because of the opposition, unexpectedly violent, which developed in the East Bay. Why should Oakland, as a city and seaport, be any less famous than San Francisco? Why, indeed? Who can say? Yet it was—and, for that matter it still is, despite the fact that in tonnage of shipping it has far outstripped San Francisco.

Since San Mateo County had supported the plan, the logical next step, after the failure of the Bay Area boroughs idea, was for San Francisco to seek a union of some kind with this friendly neighbor to the south. If anyone could bring off such a merger, Mayor "Sunny Jim" Rolph should have been the man. A native San Franciscan, well known for his business connections and social standing, he was also a master of personal showmanship.

On occasion, he could give the frivolous impression that his greatest concern was for the ever-present gardenia in his lapel, or over the question of whether the dome of his City Hall was, in fact, a few inches higher than that of the State Capitol in Sacramento. But as proof that he could also use his personal charm for important purposes, witness the fact that four times in succession he was elected Mayor of San Francisco and, after eighteen years in that position, he moved up to the governorship of California.

But even Jimmy Rolph failed to break the city's imprisoning barriers. A constitutional amendment, framed to please both San Francisco and Oakland, was passed in 1914, and Mayor Rolph tried in the Legislature of 1915 to get an enabling act passed to permit the holding of an election on the question of annexing the entire County of San Mateo to the City and County of San Francisco. Rolph got some criticism for this "unilateral" action, so the next year, when the great Panama-Pacific International Exposition was over and a pronounced success, he tried a new approach by arranging a conference with the mayors of San Mateo County's seven incorporated cities.

County officials, having a personal vested interest involved, would be hard to deal with, but the mayors might be persuaded to support his plan if he could convince them that the contemplated borough system of annexation would conserve the established rights and powers of incorporated cities.

He was to learn that the Peninsula newspapers also presented a problem, for they too had a certain vested interest in the status quo. The *San Mateo County Gazette* in Redwood City, for example, or the *San Mateo County News* in San Mateo, would certainly lose some face, if nothing more, should San Mateo County cease to exist. Or even a paper with a localized name such as the *Burlingame Advance,* in the absence of any compelling need for annexation, could be expected to raise the issue of local independence.

It was June 28, 1916 when, at Mayor Rolph's invitation, the seven mayors from San Mateo County met for a chat in his City Hall office. As reported in the San Francisco newspapers, the occasion was an exceedingly cordial one, making it appear that everybody was happy to consider a plan of union. But the Peninsula newspapers complained that this was hardly a correct appraisal of the position taken by their mayors.

Mayor Rolph told them he had no prepared program, but that he wanted the reaction of his guests to a plan of annexation in which the incorporated cities would retain their rights of self government, including the right to levy their own taxes. The only over-all taxing would be for the support of the general county government. He had in mind, he said, the organization of a committee to study the proposal, consisting of twenty representatives of the cities and the County of San Mateo and three to speak for San Francisco.

To such a committee there could be no serious objection, and the Rev. W. A. Brewer, Mayor of Hillsborough and Rector of St. Paul's Episcopal Church in Burlingame, undertook to state what he expected would be the general attitude down the Peninsula. At the moment it seemed to him that San Francisco was proposing something like a marriage. He could not but say "this is so sudden"; he and his colleagues would require time to consider the proposal.

Dr. Brewer felt, however, assuming good will on both sides, that there would be no difficulty in working out details about taxation, water supply etc., but that the paramount issue would be transportation for commuters. To win support down the Peninsula for any annexation plan, San Francisco would have to offer a commuting service as fast and as reasonable in rates as the train-and-ferry system that then served the East Bay cities. It appeared, he thought, that the Southern Pacific Company did not value its suburban business very highly, and the electric cars were too slow. Hence, the way was open, and the need was great, for a new rapid transit system.

To this, Mayor E. H. Sampson of Redwood City added a bill of particulars. To bring the commuters closer to their offices, instead of dropping them at the far-out Third-and-Townsend depot, there would need to be an elevated railway through the congested parts of the city. From downtown the new line could use the Twin Peaks Tunnel, which was then under construction. The fast transit system must, at least, reach Redwood City; a surface line would do, provided there were no grade crossings. He made the point also—which, perhaps, was the understatement of the day—that the people of Redwood City would not like the idea of losing the County courthouse.

Following this meeting there was unnecessary delay, or so it seemed, in naming the representatives for the twenty-member study committee. The County Board of Supervisors did nothing at all; the County Clerk merely advised Mayor Rolph that his letter had been received by the Board and "filed temporarily". Six cities named their men, but Mayor W. H. Pearson of Burlingame, who seemed to be dragging his feet, said he was having trouble getting someone to serve.

And there was damaging publicity down the Peninsula. The newspapers there displayed conspicuously a cartoon taken from the *Brooklyn Eagle* in which Manhattan and Brooklyn, represented as two men having dinner together, were being served very unequal portions, indicating that under the borough system, Brooklyn, due to its smaller representation on the Board of Estimate, was not getting fair treatment. The bold-type caption in the local papers was, "What annexation did to Brooklyn it might do to San Mateo County".

At the same time the Hillsborough Town Council met and announced its unanimous opposition to annexation in any form, and the members volunteered their several opinions. H. T. Scott, for example, was quoted as saying, "San Francisco has just about exhausted its power to issue bonds, and, of course, it would cherish San Mateo County as a part of it as it could then issue $50,000,000 worth of bonds on the annexed territory's assets." They all voiced the opinion that their town was happy in its present status and they could see nothing to be gained by annexation.

Dennis O'Keefe, who lived in Menlo Park and published the *San Mateo County Gazette* in Redwood City, warned against the proposal but admitted he was worried because "everybody was talking about it", and judging by his own poll of the voters in Menlo Park, he believed they favored it in a ratio of about three-to-two.

The man who master-minded the defeat of annexation at this time was Arthur H. Redington. A descendant of the Peninsula's original Howard-Poett family, he was then a practicing attorney in San Francisco, living in Hillsborough and serving there as the town's legal counsel. He it was who advised incorporating the town of Hillsborough to prevent being swallowed up by Burlingame, and to him this proposal from San Francisco was another threat to the country-club way of life that he and his neighbors wished to enjoy.

He centered his attack on the proposed borough system. He could find nothing in the law, he said, that would guarantee the rights of boroughs against the possibility that, once established as parts of a greater city-and-county system, their powers might be voted away from them by the larger body. Hence, he advised, the first thing to do was to campaign for a State Constitutional amendment to protect those rights. Whether he actually saw here a real danger or merely devised this attack as a lawyer's diversionary maneuver cannot be known, but more important is the fact that his strategy was successful in defeating the borough plan.

When Mayor Rolph succeeded in getting another meeting with Peninsula people (November 10, 1916), Redington was there to hammer away at the borough system as something that nobody really understood; therefore, it was dangerous. Speaking for the plan was Hamilton Bauer, a San Mateo attorney who had organized an Annexation League in San Mateo County, but most of the Peninsula men present, the mayors and their appointees, seemed to be saying that nothing in the proposals up to that point tempted them to consider changing their present status.

When the State legislative session opened in January, the center of contention was shifted to Sacramento. There Assemblyman Frank S. Eksward of San Mateo was ready with a bill for a constitutional amendment, probably written by Redington, providing that if a city became a self-governing borough in a larger city-and-county, its rights of self-government could not be reduced or taken away without its own voted consent. He hoped to win priority for his bill over the enabling act that was to be introduced by the annexationists.

Meanwhile, on the home front, on January 6, there was an important meeting in Burlingame, attended by some thirty people from various parts of the county, to organize a League to Preserve San Mateo County. Chosen President of this League was Judge Edward F. Fitzpatrick of Redwood City and its membership covered the Peninsula. It was designed to be a counter force to Bauer's Annexation League, but its immediate strategic objective was to prevent passage of an enabling act until a constitutional amendment could be adopted safeguarding the powers of boroughs.

As the legislative session advanced and the measures affecting the county came up for hearings, the Preservation League began to play its role. In mid-March a special train was chartered and a reported hundred people went to Sacramento for the hearing.

This demonstration of strength had the desired effect. The legislative representatives of San Francisco soon got together in Sacramento with those of San Mateo County and worked out an agreement neatly tying up the whole affair. A clause would be added to the enabling act providing that the act would not become operative until the people had approved the proposed constitutional amendment. This was done, and both measures went through to final passage.

The new provision in the enabling act meant that everything must now wait a year and a half until the next general election, when Redington's amendment would appear on the ballot. But that year-and-a-half turned out to be a longish and an earth-shaking period—it embraced for the United States the whole of its participation in the First World War! The election (November, 1918), with the by-then-forgotten amendment, was held amidst tense expectations of an armistice with Germany, and when one was actually signed, the whole country went wild with the enthusiasm of victory. Who cared then about the petty proposition on the California ballot?

The record shows that the amendment guaranteeing the rights of boroughs had carried by a margin of less than 8,000 in a total vote of 351,000, with San Mateo County voting two-to-one in favor and San Francisco strongly opposed. Legally the way was now open for the calling of an election but interest in it had become so far eclipsed by other events that nothing at all was done.

After some five years of post-war adjustments, the matter of annexation came up again—but this time (July 27, 1923), to everybody's surprise, the proposal originated down the Peninsula. When the Three Cities Chamber of Commerce, Burlingame, Hillsborough, and San Mateo, asked for a conference with the San Francisco Chamber of Commerce on the subject of "amalgamation" with San Francisco, the news even crowded the doings of President Harding out of the headlines. The President was at the moment visiting British Columbia en route from Alaska to San Francisco where, after a brief illness, he died.

For another eyebrow-raiser, the proposal at this time would annex only the northerly portion of San Mateo County, down to a line running between Belmont and San Carlos, leaving the rest of the county to shift for itself. And whereas, under the previous plans, San Francisco, being the instigator, presumably stood to gain some advantages by their adoption, in this case the people down the Peninsula were frankly asking for something.

This northern portion of the county, their argument ran, was potentially on the verge of a great industrial development, lacking only certain capital investments to bring it about. Furthermore, this most populous and urban area was acknowledged to be by nature a part of San Francisco and if it could be joined politically as well, San Francisco capital would then be available to put over the great leap forward.

Specifically, the plan called for: a borough system of government as before proposed; development at San Mateo of a port for sea-going ships, and a railroad from there to Half Moon Bay (the Ocean Shore Railroad had ceased operation in 1920); and extension of the San Francisco Municipal Railway's electric car service to Belmont, with feeder lines in San Mateo and Burlingame. The electric line then operating to San Mateo was owned by the Market Street Railway Company.

After the first burst of publicity over this proposal, there was a singular dearth of news on the subject. Apparently, San Francisco investors did not come running, with checkbooks at the ready, to finance a port at San Mateo that would compete with San Francisco's existing facilities. There was a delayed statement from the San Francisco Chamber of Commerce that it would do everything it could to aid the "cause of consolidation", and then—silence.

There was discussion, however, down the Peninsula. The Menlo Park Chamber got in its word: if there was to be a merger, Menlo should be included. And Arthur H. Redington was on hand again to debate the question with Daniel C. Imboden, Director of the Three Cities Chamber, at a meeting that was reported to be "unusually well attended" by an audience which seemed to be "about equally divided" on the subject.

Perhaps most significant was a meeting in Burlingame of the old San Mateo County Preservation League. Reorganized and ready for action, if needed, the League announced its intention to go into action, if and when the Three Cities Chamber of Commerce and the San Francisco Chamber agreed to recommend annexation. Apparently no such agreement was ever reached.

In November there was a four-man debate at a meeting of the American Legion, with Imboden and C. N. Kirkbride opposed by Redington and Horace Amphlett. Major (later Colonel) Kirkbride spoke not so much for the specific proposals then under discussion as for annexation in general. He charged those who stood stubbornly for the status quo, just to keep their own taxes down, with a large measure of responsibility for causing San Francisco to lose its status as California's busiest seaport, whereas Los Angeles and Long Beach, by cooperating with each other, had surged ahead to take first rank.

Interest in the Three Cities' visionary proposal gradually waned; in fact the Three Cities Chamber itself, as an attempt at inter-city unity, was not succeeding. Its name was a misnomer because Hillsborough as a town had no commercial interests. It was finally replaced by separate chambers of commerce in Burlingame and San Mateo.

But interest in some kind of merger with San Francisco did not die. Just how strong was that sentiment will never be accurately known, but in 1927-28 the effort to attain a union entered a new and more serious phase than any previously undertaken. It began with an attempt to gather, in a competent and professional manner, a body of factual information. The San Francisco Bureau of Government, financed by the city Chamber of Commerce, undertook a survey of San Francisco and San Mateo County, but more particularly the latter, compiling all the facts which might need to be considered in planning a program of annexation.

In 1928, this factual material regarding such matters as government, highways, school systems, special districts and property values was published in a 200-page book, at a cost, for compiling and printing, of upwards of $20,000. When compiled, the very bulk and complexity of the assembled information must have tended to discourage those who were working for consolidation.

This feeling was reflected at a meeting in Burlingame High School after the

*Survey* had been published. About 300 people came out to hear W. H. Manry who had directed the study. He was candid and forthright in saying the process of achieving consolidation was difficult and that he was not at all certain that the course of procedure suggested in the *Survey* was the best one. He outlined other things that might be done—all of them difficult.

Present also was San Francisco's great City Engineer, M. W. O'Shaughnessy, creator of the Hetch Hetchy water system and a towering personality who was likened to San Francisco's Twin Peaks. He spoke with refreshing frankness of highway projects (Bayshore and Junipero Serra) then added, "We hurried these along, not because we love you so much but because we want to have roads for our motorists to get in and out of the city".

The meeting broke up with everybody in high good humor but with no clear idea of what should come next. Within a few days, a Committee of Ten was appointed, five each from San Francisco and San Mateo County, to study the *Survey* and try to work out a way to use its findings for the desired purpose. The committee, and particularly a legal sub-committee headed by C. N. Kirkbride, put in months of effort on this task.

Studying the items, one by one, they came to the schools. San Francisco's Superintendent, Dr. Joseph Marr Gwinn, saw no problem—the Peninsula's schools could be easily absorbed into the city system. But San Mateo County's Superintendent of Schools, Miss Pansy Jewett Abbott, presented a different picture. She cannily suggested to the Committee that they hold a meeting with the district superintendents of the county, and a date was set for such a meeting.

But it does not appear that this meeting ever came off. Probably not. To ask ten men for their opinions on a project that would abolish their jobs would hardly seem necessary. And what about the forty-two elected boards of trustees that governed the schools in cities, villages, and rural communities, all of which would presumably be abolished? Or the people who voted for the men and women to govern their schools?

Experts could argue convincingly that consolidation of schools under one district management would improve the quality of education as well as reduce the cost, and history shows that rural people can be persuaded to consolidate their districts for greater efficiency. But to talk of having all the schools of all the county's districts put into one package, stripped of their locally elected boards, and together with their PTA's and all of the other intimate neighborhood activities that surround them, dropped into the hands of a huge, foreign, and impersonal city system? This would require some persuading!

The annexationists finally gave up; at precisely what point it is impossible to say, but it is easy to see why they gave up. One might reason that the opposition, though obviously strong, could be beaten in a straight yes-or-no vote on annexation, but it was not that simple. Not only was there Redington's amendment to the Constitution, but in 1922 another roadblock had been thrown in the way. All in all, a legal opinion that outlined the steps now required for annexation listed four separate elections that must be held. First, the cities of San Mateo County would vote; next the unincorporated areas; and then, the county as a whole. Finally, if the plan survived all this, San Francisco would vote. If any of the Peninsula's cities voted against annexation, and the rest of the county voted for it, those cities would become independent municipalities, or "floating islands", as someone put it, surrounded by city-and-county. Alternative plans were suggested but each had its serious drawbacks.

In the face of all these complications, the whole matter went by the board and was almost forgotten—but not entirely. The basic need that had prompted all these strivings for unity had not been satisfied. Hence, we may expect that, one day, Necessity, that ancient mother of invention, will inspire someone to finally come up with a workable plan to fill this void.

But future proposals, we may be sure, will be called by some new name—not merely because "annexation" has become a bad word, but because the economy of the Bay Area, and particularly of this Peninsula, is now undergoing another profound change. Once a hinterland for San Francisco, producer of its food and lumber and buyer of its merchandise, then a suburb with bedrooms and gardens for its tired executives, it is clearly now becoming something else—something like a co-equal segment of a great urban and industrial complex.

In a recent five-year period, the number of people commuting into San Francisco during the morning rush hours increased by 27%, but the number during the same hours going in the *opposite direction* increased by 58%; people commuting from the City to jobs down the Peninsula!

This is only one symptom of what is going on. Traffic across the Bay, in both directions, has grown so much as to require doubling the capacity of the San Mateo-Hayward Bridge. Industrial employment in San Mateo County, 1950 to 1958, increased by 70%, as compared to San Francisco's 4%. During the same eight years wholesale trade in San Mateo County increased 816%, a far greater increase than in any other Bay county. In the year 1960, new industrial plants and new units added to old ones in San Mateo County numbered 292—six times as many as in 1950.

Another interesting evidence of growth is the telephone. The telegraph first came to the Peninsula in 1852, the railroad in 1863, and the telephone in 1883. The telegraph has since bowed out, the railroad is on the decline, but the telephone grows ever more vigorously. In 1950, 62,790 phones were listed in San Mateo County; in 1959 there were 147,364, and in 1961 the total was 156,352.

The attitude toward industries has undergone a complete about-face; towns that formerly fought them off, fearing they would down-grade their status as high-class residential, now advertise their industrial parks where they are inviting selected kinds of industry to come in and help bear the tax load. All this is leading into a new situation that cannot fail to affect, in more ways than one, San Mateo County's relationships with our neighbors in the Bay Area.

The Peninsula has had some local industries ever since the beginning of American village life—in addition, that is, to the grist mills and blacksmith shops that in those days were found everywhere. A most interesting example of this, because it was a natural development in this area, was the business of tanning; cowhides were available from the ranches and local butchers, tan oak grew abundantly in the hills, and there was a good California market for leather.

As early as the 1850's there were two tanneries in Redwood City, which changed ownership a few times, but although the conditions that favored their beginning changed, the Beeger Tannery did not close until the 1930's, and the Frank Tannery held on until the 1950's. By that time, however, tan bark was brought from Mendocino County and even from Oregon, hides were obtained through dealers from far and near, and the market for the specialized kinds of leather then produced was world-wide.

In recent times the most striking industrial development has been in the field of electronics. This is the type of industry that is welcomed even by towns that are known to be mainly residential; and being dependent for its progress on scientific research, it thrives in the atmosphere surrounding a great university.

In 1955 the Palo Alto Historical Association published a study of electronic research and production in this area. Omitting from the list the radio broadcasting stations and the laboratories of Stanford University itself, the study named 36 firms in the business, one of which was in San Bruno, two in Belmont, eight in San Carlos, six in Redwood City, five in Menlo Park, and fourteen in Palo Alto.

The impressive story, told in sober statements of fact, accounts for many basic inventions such as the Audion Amplifier and the mobile two-way radio telephone. It is also replete with Horatio Alger-like tales of great inventions made in garages, and of back-yard laboratories that developed into million-dollar production firms.

Seven years later (1962) the total number of electronic firms in the same area had increased from 36 to 152. There was then at least one firm in every town that would permit them from South San Francisco to Mountain View, but the greatest growth was in the cities of Palo Alto (new total 78), Redwood City (17), and San Carlos (14). There were 39 firms with more than a hundred employees each, and seven that employed more than a thousand. The grand total of employees working in electronics was approximately 30,750.

The periodical, *Industrial Development* (October, 1962), summarized recent growth in San Mateo and Santa Clara counties as follows: "The new industrial empire that has grown up here in the last 30 years is different from any other in the United States, although there are similarities with the Boston complex on the other side of the continent. The electronics and related industries are more nearly dominant here than elsewhere in the country, although there is a respectable amount of other industry, some of it quite unrelated.

"The outstanding characteristics of the area's industry are the dominance of technology, the seminal role played by Stanford University, and the selective attraction that the local environment has exerted on hard-to-find scientific and technical specialists and the absence of many of the problems that have plagued other industrial areas."

Business and industry in San Mateo County are bringing us to the end of an era. No longer is the Peninsula a mere suburb of San Francisco. Will it come to have a balanced economy all its own? Will the future, through electronics and related industries, lead to stronger ties with the growing industrial complex in Santa Clara County?

Meanwhile San Mateo County, and its biggest neighbor, the City and County of San Francisco, continue in the old ways of "getting on" with each other, and not doing too badly at it, considering that San Francisco is more intimately linked with the Peninsula than with any other part of the Bay Area. And this is not evading the fact that now and again the two, in their communications with each other, drop to the juvenile level—like small brothers and sisters who are polite enough to outsiders but turn their meanest snarls on each other.

These intimate and tangled relationships are worthy of some study. One subject that can be depended upon any time to furnish material for a discussion is the extraordinary system of water supply, under which, through a series of fortuitous circumstances, the City-and-County of San Francisco has been cast in the role of an entrepreneur in the business of bringing water from the distant High Sierra and selling it to the Peninsula communities; while San Mateo County, on the other hand, levies taxes on San Francisco's vast lands and reservoirs that lie within its borders.

The best way to explain this odd situation is to tell how it all happened. The familiar place name, Spring Valley, did not originate in our beautiful valley of lakes, as many people suppose, but in a small one, now in the concrete heart of San Francisco. It was there that the Spring Valley Water Company began. It later reached for more water down the Peninsula, starting in a small way by building the Pilarcitos Dam, hidden in the hills, and carrying the water by gravity, in a thirty-two mile redwood flume, from there to the City. This system was completed in the fiscal year 1862-63.

The genius in the later part of this story was Hermann Schussler, a young German engineer whose monument may be seen at the concrete dam on Skyline Boulevard. Employed by the company in 1864, Schussler guided the company to an expansion of its watershed holdings and its dams until it brought under control practically all of the run-off water on the higher levels in the northern half of the Peninsula.

Schussler's first job was the building of the San Andreas Dam (1868) and, ten years later, he constructed the Old Crystal Springs Dam, which is now a causeway between two lakes. It was built to impound the waters of Laguna Creek by creating what is now the most southerly of the Crystal Springs lakes.

The final and crowning part of Schussler's catchment system was the concrete Crystal Springs Dam across the throat of San Mateo Creek. This involved, for those times, a remarkable feat of long-range planning as well as an engineering triumph. First the farms in the valley were quietly purchased, as well as the famous old Crystal Springs Hotel in the shady depths of the narrow ravine. As the buildings were razed and the brush cleared away, the actual construction began in 1887. When the dam was completed, three years later, it was visited and viewed with admiration by engineers from everywhere, and was publicized as the world's largest cement dam.

More important than this, however, was the fact that it stood the test of the 1906 earthquake. Pipes that lay across the San Andreas Fault, which by-passes the dam only a few hundred feet away, were sheared in two or thrown out of the ground as the land mass shifted along the fault. The road and fence that crossed it on the causeway were parted and left with an eight- or nine-foot offset. Yet the strength

San Mateo County industries featured at San Francisco's "Midwinter Fair," 1894.

Workmen in Frank's Tannery, Redwood City, 1885.

Redwood City, southwest corner of Main and Broadway, in the
1880's.

Leslie Salt, San Mateo

Western Meat Company (1915), South San Francisco's first industry.

The "Reichardt Duck Farm," South San Francisco, 1915.

Crystal Springs Dam, 1890, and Hermann
Schussler, the engineer who planned and
built it.

Concrete-mixing machinery at work on Crystal Springs, "largest cement dam in the world."

and flexibility of this large dam brought it through all this shaking without any damage.

It was composed of many blocks of concrete, separately poured, varying in shape and size—roughly they were six to ten feet high, up to forty feet long, and ten to fifteen feet wide. All were cast in irregular, interlocking geometric shapes. The dam as a whole, when completed, was 145 feet high.

As the population of San Francisco increased it became evident that the Peninsula alone could not supply the city's future needs for water. The company developed more sources in Alameda County but the city itself began to look farther afield—to California's Sierra Nevada Mountains. In the year 1900 a new city charter was adopted which contained provisions for a municipally owned water system, and under this authority studies were made of possible sources in that far-away area.

After these studies had resulted in the selection of a portion of the Tuolumne River system in Yosemite National Park, which came to be known as Hetch Hetchy, there followed a long series of negotiations with different branches of the Federal Government for permission to construct necessary dams and conduits and to withdraw water for San Francisco's needs from this government property.

The culmination was the passing of the Raker Act, which secured the necessary rights to San Francisco. It was signed by President Woodrow Wilson on December 19, 1913. In the meantime, San Francisco had voted two bond issues totalling $45,600,-000 and had adopted a plan for withdrawal of up to 400,000,000 gallons of water daily, to be carried by gravity to the Bay Area. The plan also included development of extensive plants for hydro-electric power.

Efforts to plan a single water-supply system for all the Bay Area cities had been made, but this had fallen through along with the collapse of the Greater San Francisco proposal. The East Bay cities had to build their own parallel system, bringing water also from the High Sierra.

While San Francisco's Hetch Hetchy system was a-building, the next important step was to acquire the facilities of the Spring Valley Water Company in order to form a wholly municipal system. After long negotiations over the price, and after one attempt to vote bonds had failed, finally, in 1928, San Francisco bonded itself for another $41,000,000 and, on March 3, 1930, the city officials took over all the properties and facilities of the Spring Valley Water Company in the city and down the Peninsula. From here on, in matters of taxes and permits, and the price to be paid for water, the County of San Mateo had to deal not with a private company that was subject to state regulations but with its neighbor, the City and County of San Francisco.

When the pipes from Yosemite were all laid over the hills and across the Bay, and an ornamental Pulgas Temple had been built where the crystal mountain water came to its destination in the Crystal Springs Lakes, everyone on the Peninsula, as well as in San Francisco, was made aware of a historic event on October 24, 1934, when the sound of the first gurgling water coming through the Temple was broadcast by radio throughout the land.

The importance of this event has been magnified with the passing years. The doubling and re-doubling of the Peninsula's population has made all of the Peninsular cities increasingly dependent on this source of water. Local wells that once were adequate have become insignificant or have been abandoned because of their lowering of the water table, and the City and County of San Francisco has become the water merchant for the entire Peninsula.

On March 3, 1960, the thirtieth anniversary of the City's taking possession of its water system, the San Francisco Water Department released statistics to show that its capital investment in local property and facilities had increased from the original $41 million to $107 million, besides about $300 million in the Hetch Hetchy system. Most interesting, perhaps, was the fact that of all the 103 million gallons of water per day delivered to users, 62 million gallons (60%) go to suburban customers. The Department pays its way, and the water is unsurpassed in quality.

Other "utility" services (gas and electricity) are also shared with neighboring counties, but instead of becoming municipally owned, these have remained in the hands of private enterprise. Historical information about them is meager, but we find familiar Peninsula names among the promoters. Peter Donahue, in 1854, lighted the muddy street-corners of San Francisco with gas jets. By the late 1870's, electric lights were an exciting new curiosity as well as a new kind of business enterprise. In September, 1879, sputtering arc lamps were turned on for the first time in San Francisco, three years ahead of New York City. Ten years later, when long-distance transmission lines were found to be practicable, Redwood City enjoyed the same experience.

Among Peninsula personalities in this new line of business was Prince Andre Poniatowski, brother-in-law to William H. Crocker, and builder of the canyon home in Hillsborough known as Skyfarm. Another was Eugene de Sabla, who lived, at the turn of the century, in "El Cerrito", the former home of William D. M. Howard. It was a group of capitalists headed by de Sabla who in 1905 founded a corporation under the name of Pacific Gas and Electric Company—the firm that now serves most of northern California.

The most admired of San Francisco's facilities in San Mateo County, yet the one that has occasioned the loudest and angriest protests, is the International Airport. Its screaming jets have deafened neighboring residents by day and awakened them at night, and they in turn have screamed, at city council meetings and through the press, making dire threats of action to be taken about it. But when the newspapers carried a hint that the entire airport might move across the Bay, taking its travel service and its huge payroll with it, the sudden silence was almost as audible as the screams had been. Efforts by the airport management to abate the nuisance, and adjustments made in the neighboring cities, have from time to time, relieved tensions, but by no means have all of the problems been solved.

Ever since its beginning in 1927, Mills Field, as it was first called, has been a center of interest down the Peninsula. Old timers still thrill to the memory of Charles Lindbergh's *Spirit of Saint Louis* circling in for a landing, shortly after it had made its famous flight to Paris. They also feel, once again, the chagrin they experienced two years later when "Lindy" came for a second visit, this time with a heavy plane, and the news was flashed around the world that "at San Francisco Airport Lindbergh's plane got stuck in the mud".

However, during that same week in 1929, it was noticed with amazement that 591 flights were made to and from the field, carrying, in all, 902 passengers. This was recorded as a "busy week". Late in 1961, however, passengers were averaging more than 15,000 a day.

San Francisco at first leased the land for the airport from the heirs of D. O. Mills, and named it Mills Field in the hope that the owners would donate at least a part of the purchase price. But when it became clear that no such thing could be expected, the people of San Francisco bonded themselves to buy the land and changed the name to San Francisco International Airport.

As a major hub of air-passenger traffic, this airport was rated in 1960 as fifth in the world, but for expanding and modernizing its facilities, and for pioneering in design and in new conveniences for travelers, it has been consistently out in front as one of the world's leaders.

San Mateo County also shares with its neighbors the problems of surface transportation. Profound changes taking place in this field are heralded by the rapid shift in recent years from ferry boats to bridges and from rails to freeways. Planners are driven frantic by everybody's insistence on traveling only in his own car, and on driving it wherever and whenever he jolly well pleases.

Four bridges now connect the Peninsula with lands across salt water. A beginning was made with the Dumbarton Bridge in 1925, and the San Mateo-Hayward Bridge followed in 1929. This structure was built of cement made in Redwood City from oyster shells taken from the Bay itself. The great San Francisco-Oakland Bridge was completed in 1936, and the Golden Gate Bridge, chaste and beautiful, its lace-like cables forming "harps for the winds of Heaven", was proudly dedicated in 1937. Four great bridges were constructed in a dozen remarkable years.

On land, the Peninsula is destined by its very nature—with a large city at its northward tip—to have an ever-acute problem of roads. Five arterials that now bear traffic up and down the Peninsula were built largely piece by piece but more or less in this order: first there was El Camino Real; then the Coast Highway (California No. 1); followed by Skyline Boulevard; and, lastly, Junípero Serra Boulevard and the Bayshore Freeway. But, for the future, there is still talk of the need for more roads as well as for more bridges.

As to rails, the Southern Pacific Company has seen its commuter service rise and decline. The electric line that began a parallel service in 1903 was brought to an end and its tracks torn up after fifty years of indifferent success. Highways, meantime, have increased in number and capacity but new roads are choked with traffic as soon as they are completed.

Study of this baffling problem has not been wanting. A San Francisco Bay Area Rapid Transit Commission spent six years gathering facts and weighing various possible solutions. Then in 1957 the State Legislature created the San Francisco Bay Area Rapid Transit District, a special-purpose regional authority with taxing powers, and embracing five counties: San Francisco, Marin, San Mateo, Alameda, and

Contra Costa. Its activities were headed by a sixteen-member Board of Directors, whose members were chosen by mayors and boards of supervisors in the five member counties.

This Board, after careful study, like the Commission that preceded it, could find no better solution to the problem than to build a new system of rails with modern high-speed electric trains, running from underground stations in San Francisco to the various outlying cities of the Bay Area.

This proposed system, to cost an estimated $1,025,000,000, must first be approved by the boards of supervisors in the member counties; then to activate it, the people must approve by a 60% majority vote the issuing of general-obligation bonds to finance the undertaking.

Thus the ultimate decision, whether or not to undertake this great venture, was put up to the people. Would this proposed system in the long years ahead, be worth the money? The automobile has lured commuters and shoppers away from public transportation; can trains, shiny new and rapid, lure them back?

Two counties said no in advance, and one of them was San Mateo. Marin County was stopped in part by the question, on which engineering authorities disagreed, as to whether the Golden Gate Bridge could safely carry a railroad and trains. In San Mateo County, the Board of Supervisors decided to withdraw from the District because it seemed to them very doubtful whether the proposed new system, which on the Peninsula must run parallel to existing facilities, could possibly improve upon the present service enough to justify the heavy investment. The matter was left over for continuing study, however, and some attempt has been made to view it in conjunction with Santa Clara County.

The electorate in the remaining three (San Francisco and the two East Bay counties) voted "yes" on November 6, 1962, by a sufficient majority to authorize the building of a transit system for them alone. The outcome of the plans will be watched with great interest, not only by San Mateo and Marin counties, but by other large cities everywhere.

The water system and the Airport are by no means all of the institutions maintained by San Francisco in San Mateo County. There is the County Jail and its accompanying farm at San Bruno, and the Log Cabin Ranch at La Honda, a rehabilitation center for boys in trouble. Altogether, for the fiscal year 1961, San Francisco paid to San Mateo County in property taxes the considerable sum of $638,795.74.

Things are indeed "mixed up" on the Peninsula, and naturally so, for even with all of it taken together, throwing in the city of San Francisco, it is a smallish place. On this same Peninsula where the Spanish missionaries and army men argued with each other about room for themselves and their cattle, when there were less than 1,500 people, white and Indian, and not over 5,000 head of livestock, there are in 1963 a million and a half people with all their cats and dogs, 10,000 cattle, sheep, and riding horses, besides a game preserve with something like 1500 deer and a few coyotes.

And there is still this "unbreakable barrier" that in certain legal aspects is supposed to divide this small area into two tightly sealed compartments, but over which a great human tide daily ebbs and flows. Even the people who live astride it have always found ways of not letting it interfere with their lives, any more than if they lived on the Equator. The Spaniards argued over grazing land; today's inhabitants argue over jet planes, and so the good neighbor relationships are carried on.

Perhaps, after all, even the bottling up of San Francisco may not be altogether bad. Can anyone imagine trying to spread "The City's" unique charms over an area, say, the size of Los Angeles? And despite boundary lines and local rivalries, there are unquestionably strong sentimental ties that draw the Bay Area together. The various cities and even the remote suburbs bask freely in the reflected fame of the City by the Golden Gate; they all like to be thought of as "very San Francisco".

# X. Heritage: *The past that is still with us*

*"How would we know it's us without our past?"*  A Junior Historian

### Bequests from Mother Nature

San Franciscans write odes to the fog, their famous built-in air conditioner that on rare hot days comes creeping softly in "on little cat feet", while the people of San Mateo County get just as sentimental, if not as eloquent, about their warm sunshine. The Golden Gate is not only a passage for water; it is also a gap where two giant masses of air meet in constant combat—the one from the ocean cool and moisture-laden, the other hot and dry from the inland. Hence this famous gateway creates its own brand of climate, which blankets the land nearby.

And just below the city-and-county line another gateway stands open, not for the ocean but for its winds, that sweep unhindered through to the Bay. Here a story was born that tells how the town of Colma is alleged to have come by its uncommon name. When the railroad was new and the trains from the Peninsula's sunshine belt stopped at the Schoolhouse Station, which was then its name, and stood with car doors open to the wind and fog, children among the passengers crept close to their mothers and were heard to say, "It's col(d) Ma!".

But in this land of no extremes, the relative terms "cold" and "hot" have a regional meaning. The season that is elsewhere called winter here brings temperatures in the fifties, with an occasional frosty night, and a yearly rainfall of some 20 inches. Summer, on the other hand, though rainless, is refreshed by temperatures in the sixties and seventies, with only rare days when the mercury gets pushed as high as ninety.

Then there are the hills, which also affect the climate. Strangers who are sensitive to weather, and who want to enjoy outdoor living, should never be hasty in choosing a homesite in San Mateo County, for often, by moving only a mile or so in any direction, or perhaps behind a sheltering hill, they can find a spot much more to their liking than the first they select.

Peninsula dwellers who have guests from out of county are pretty sure to entertain them with a ride to see the country. Invariably, after only minutes on the road, the guests exclaim at the beauty of a canyon drive or the view from a hilltop: "What? All this so close to home?" And probably the next surprise is when the Crystal Springs Lakes flash into view. You tell the truth, of course; they are reservoirs, or "our water supply", but no less beautiful for being a utility and man-made.

If the host knows a little history, he can add enormously to the interest by pointing out from the Crystal Springs Dam and Schussler Monument, "Over there is the drowned valley of San Mateo Creek; here before us was once a valley of farms—the stagecoaches came through this gap and around the point to the right was a famous resort hotel called Crystal Springs which gave the valley its name, and yonder to the left was the Laguna District School and another resort . . . ."

The wise host will not fail to show his friend the Coastside, beginning perhaps with the spectacular Point San Pedro at the foot of Montara Mountain, with its crags and curving strata, and quiet Shelter Cove; then, by contrast, close by, the Devil's Slide down which many a foolhardy fisherman or would-be mountain climber has ventured (it looks easy from the top), only to find that getting back (*if* he got back!) was impossible without help from the County Sheriff or the Coast Guard.

Then comes the Bay of the Half Moon, enclosed today by a new breakwater in addition to its sheltering Pillar Point, which has had a succession of pillars at its point. Little by little, the sea has forced it back—carving out pillars by eroding the soft spots, then knocking down the pillars. This little game has left in its wake not only a protruding reef, but in the pre-breakwater years, caused more and more of the coastline behind the Point to succumb to the action of the sea. The road paralleling the beach has twice, in a quarter-century, had to be moved back.

All the marvels of the sea are there. Both south and north along the San Mateo coast are reefs with mirror-like tide pools inviting a study of sea life; there are sandy beaches and fishing rocks, and the once famous Pebble Beach, source of semi-precious stones. Finally, at the county line is the chalky mountain that through the years, since Portolá came in 1769, forced travelers to go down to the wet sand even though the county, each year, when the rains were over, rebuilt the road. Until World War II this went on. Then the United States Government, facing the very possible necessity of having to move troops along the coast to resist invasion, literally removed the face of the mountain and cast it into the sea. Thus the mountain lost its face, but its crumbling slope, though moved back, is still there.

Variety, the spice of scenery here, is endless. Driving up a mountain side, one turns a corner and suddenly is in a different world—from hot slopes covered with chaparral and manzanita one is catapulted into a grove of stately redwoods, cool and dank, the sun's rays perpetually forbidden to enter. Or from the 2,000-foot summit of King's Mountain he looks down on the Bay, the valleys and the lakes; then, with a slight shifting of position, he views the beach and the vast Pacific.

Or sitting in a restaurant, the host and his guests gaze from the window into the throat of a yawning canyon, the far bottom of it filled with mighty redwoods which, from the distance, to the viewers look like asparagus plants. Then the party stops by the roadside to inspect at close range old "Skyline Methuselah". This lone redwood, during its lifetime, has looked down upon Indian smokes, Spanish explorers

Secluded spot at Stone Dam on the upper Pilarcitos.

Searsville Lake.

San Gregorio Beach.

Lower Falls of the Bútano at high water time.

El Camino Real, historic road of the West.

and American bonanza mansions. It has weathered storms and fires, is a bit crippled, but is still as healthy as the Peninsula itself.

Or from Skegg's Point on the crest of the mountain, the party may study the Bayside build-up of modern times, swinging their gaze from the giant blimp hangar at Moffet Field to Stanford University, up the solid row of Peninsula towns to the San Bruno Mountains, and in the distance the cities of the East Bay.

Before his guests go home our host will undoubtedly hope for a chance to show them one of the spectacular acts that nature puts on at times, but seems to reserve for special occasions—times when the mighty atmospheric battle being fought high above the Peninsula's central ridge becomes sharply visible.

The cool ocean air rises over the ridge but there is met by the warm inland atmosphere, and stopped in its tracks. So, on this vertical battle plane is formed a mounting mass of billowy cloud that rises higher and higher in a stupendous, surging wall, glistening faintly in the soft daylight.

Reaching upward beyond the limit of visibility, it seems to be vainly struggling to move, while at the bottom it sends out scouting feelers down the valleys of the ridge, but none of them get very far— they end in a feathery fringe and disappear.

### Legacies from Spain and Mexico

El Camino Real is a road over which much history has traveled; from the earliest beginnings, now nearly two centuries ago, it has been a long and vital lifeline of communications between the communities along the coast.

Here on the Peninsula it has had many names: *El Camino para San Francisco,* or *para San José* as the case might be; the Old Mission Trail; Old Mission Road; the County Road; El Camino Real, and U. S. 101. But its official name now, El Camino Real, became official only in recent times, and is not as historic as many people suppose.

When Spaniards say *camino* they mean a *way* to get somewhere—anything from a trail to a boulevard. The word *real* (ray-ál) meaning royal or national, distinguishes a *public* road, officially dedicated, from a local or unofficial one. This is the main point: in the wide-spread open country of Spanish days in California there was certainly no need to dedicate a road. This camino was then merely a trail from mission to mission, through the open stretches of the public domain. Privately owned ranch land was almost unknown under Spain; the few grants that were made were use-permits rather than title deeds. Most of the land grants of historic importance were made under the Mexican Republic, and rarely if ever then, would anyone think of calling a road "royal".

Where, then, did this *"El Camino Real"* name come from? Who first suggested it is impossible to say, but the drive to popularize its use started about 1906 with the Native Sons and Daughters of the Golden West and a Mrs. A. S. C. Forbes—of Los Angeles.

This was when "touring" by automobile over winding dirt roads was becoming a brand new sport, with new thrills and special toggery—goggles, veil, duster, huge gauntlet gloves. To guide these happy wanderers and painlessly teach them some history, Mrs. Forbes designed and patented a mission-bell guide post consisting of a clapperless iron bell hung by a gooseneck from an iron pipe; a sign was attached to each one, reading *"El Camino Real"* and giving the distance in both directions to the nearest missions. Most of the missions were then in a ruined condition and none of them had yet been restored, but this at least focussed some attention on the ruins.

The idea of erecting these signs was popularized also through the El Camino Real Association, with chapters in various towns, and through many other clubs and societies which bought the bells from Mrs. Forbes and erected them along the road in their respective localities. The goal of the promoters was to have a bell for every mile over the entire length of the mission chain, and in some parts of southern California this goal was actually achieved. These hundreds of bells, it is said, were all cast in Mrs. Forbes' back yard.

The first one erected in San Mateo County was at Redwood City, in 1909, by the local chapters of the Native Daughters and Native Sons of the Golden West. There is one still doing duty by the roadside in San Mateo, at Clark Drive and El Camino, and another at Broadway in Burlingame. A few others may still be found along the highway, lost perhaps among modern street signs and telephone poles.

The road itself is a clue to history. It was not laid out in the beginning by a crew of engineers; its route was chosen by trial and error—by travelers following each others' tracks, and deviating here and there to explore for a cut-off or better terrain. Northward from Santa Clara Mission, for example, it struck out across the flat valley toward the first conspicuous landmark—the *palo alto* (tall tree) on San Francisquito Creek—and, similarly, from there to the spot where Redwood City now stands, at the head of tidewater in Redwood Creek. From there northward the route was a game of dodging between sloughs on one side and hills on the other.

After passing the hills at Belmont, there was another stretch of flat terrain, and the road made a bee-line for the Hospice, or mission outpost building, on San Mateo Creek. Travelers forded the stream about where they unconsciously cross it today on a highway bridge, and the building stood in what is now the parking lot at Baywood Avenue. This in mission days was the only building between Santa Clara and San Francisco (Dolores) missions, and it was a place to stop, if need be, over night.

The road then curved past "the Mound" on the west and continued picking its way between hills and sloughs to the vicinity of Tanforan Racetrack in San Bruno; there it no longer followed the contours of the Bay but went directly northward and crossed Colma Creek approximately at the spot where the City of South San Francisco has preserved a short section of its route in a street named Old Mission Road. It followed up the easterly side of the valley of the cemeteries, reaching the foot of the hill in the present Daly City, where it was joined (as it is today—1963) by San Pedro Road, which was then the trail from the Coastside and "Pedro Valley".

Up the slope past Jefferson High School, it went through the gap in the hill, called in Spanish times *La Portezuela* (the pass), where San José Avenue and Mission Street now meet. Even then, there was a fork in the road at this point: the direct trail to the Presidio took off in the direction of San José Avenue, and the way to the

Mission was approximately the route of Mission Street to the spot where the Mission Chapel still stands on Dolores at Sixteenth.

Newcomers here from the East may wonder at the many Spanish place-names beginning with *San*. Although perhaps familiar with *Saint* Louis, *Saint* Joe and *Saint* Lawrence, they may have failed to recognize the saints with their names in Spanish (*San* masculine and *Santa* feminine). As with the French in the Mississippi Valley, so in California the Spanish trail-blazing parties were accompanied by priests who wrote the record and who, in many instances, were probably the only literate men in the party. So in looking for names with which to label streams and other landmarks, the calendar of the saints and holy days was the source most frequently used.

Closely akin to place names is the important history of land titles. If you own any real estate in San Mateo County, your right to it probably goes back to someone who purchased a portion of one of the ranchos described in Chapter Three. If you care to look up his deed you will find a lengthy document describing the acreage by "metes and bounds". It will tell you, perhaps, to start at a stake at the westerly edge of the County Road and on the line of the property of John Jones, go thence westerly along said line to a creek, thence follow the meanders of said creek, and so on around the property to the point of beginning.

But the Mexican land grants did not cover all of San Mateo County. If your land happens to be in the Colma region, or in the mountainous area west of the Peninsula's central ridge, tracing back the ownership may lead instead to a patent issued by the United States Government Land Office. In this event, the description will follow the plan of land measurement that was born in the fertile brain of Thomas Jefferson—something like this: "The south one half of the northeast one fourth of Section Ten, Township Two South", etc. etc.

Some buyers of property in the 1850's got caught, so to speak, between the two systems. Alexander Moore, for example, the pioneer settler in Pescadero, bought land from Juan José Gonzáles, grantee of Rancho Pescadero, and had it carefully mapped on parchment. But when the U. S. surveyors finished mapping Gonzáles's grant, most of Moore's purchase lay outside its boundaries. Gonzáles, unintentionally of course, had sold land that was not his, and Moore, having put improvements on the property, had to buy it again from the U. S. Government.

One clause in Gonzáles's grant deed said "from the sea to the top of the mountains" and if taken literally this would have given him at least 50,000 acres; but another clause in the same document limited him to half a square league, which turned out to be a mere 3,282 acres.

The record of early California land titles is full of this kind of confusion; to us at this distance the incidents are a source of amusement but they were not so then to the people concerned. To some they spelled great good luck and to others tragedy.

Visible and tangible relics of Spanish-Mexican days on the Peninsula are now very rare; the only one remaining that is both authentic and available to the public is the Sánchez Adobe in the City of Pacifica.

Built of sun-dried adobe bricks, at least some of which were probably made in the 1790's for the San Pedro mission outpost, this remarkable building was completed, about as it stands today, in 1846. Despite its height of two stories, it has survived two devastating earthquakes as well as the erosion of time and use.

Francisco Sánchez, son of José and grantee of Rancho San Pedro, lived in this house from 1846, the year of the American invasion of California, until his death in 1862, except as public duties took him to the village at Mission Dolores. He was rated during these years as one of the ten wealthiest men in San Mateo County.

After Sánchez's death, his family was scattered. An American, Francis Sievers, leased the rancho and lived in the house while he sub-leased portions of the land for truck farming. Some time later the rancho was divided among various claimants; then the house and a strip of land reaching up over Montara Mountain was bought by General Edward Kirkpatrick (1879), a veteran of the Civil War. Kirkpatrick remodeled the house, added a frame structure, and landscaped the garden, making of it a very attractive home. Although he later moved to Europe, he and his widow after him held the property until the 1940's. It was then acquired by Ray Higgins and Associates, and in 1947 was purchased, with Higgins' cooperation, by the County of San Mateo.

The house, meanwhile, had been a bootleg bar in Prohibition times, and was known as a "hotel" or a "hunting lodge", euphemisms for almost anything. Its final use was as a shed for packing artichokes and as a bunk house for laborers.

In October, 1946, the County Historical Association held a centennial *merienda*, or Spanish-style picnic, at the house, which drew a large and happy crowd, and helped persuade the County Supervisors that the house should be purchased and restored as a historic monument. When the restoration was completed it was placed in the hands of the Department of Parks and Recreation for care and administration. Furnishings were purchased, in part, by the County, but most have been donated by interested individuals.

The Charles Brown Adobe in Woodside dates from Mexican times, perhaps as early as 1838, but was built by an American who married a Spanish California girl from San José. Brown also built the County's first sawmill on Alambique Creek near his house, but he later lost the property. It was purchased by Col. Jack Hays, San Francisco's popular first sheriff, who later became U. S. Surveyor General for California. Hays' biographer, James Kimmins Greer, is authority for the statement that for about a year (1851) he lived in this Woodside house and commuted daily on horseback to his office in San Francisco! Besides being a wonderful man, he must have had a wonderful horse, or perhaps he anticipated Ralston by having a relay of horses. Later owners of the house were E. W. Burr, Mayor of San Francisco, and from 1883 John A. Hooper, San Francisco banker. The historic building was cherished and restored by the Hooper family. In 1962 a portion of the property, including the adobe, was sold to Mr. and Mrs. Hannes Schroll of Palo Alto.

One more relic, a unique building on Rancho de las Pulgas, probably built to serve as a house for herdsmen, stood until 1956, on Coleman Avenue near Ringwood Road, in Menlo Park. It is a hybrid structure; like the Mexican palizada, except that instead of poles stuck in the ground, its frame is of sawed lumber—upright studdings with horizontal slats, and then the whole wall plastered full of mud and tamped solid. Reliable testimony places its origin sometime earlier than 1846, hence its framing must have been hand-sawed in the saw-pits of Woodside. When well cared for, set in a garden of flowers, it was an attractive little building.

Recently the inevitable seemed to have come: it was about to be pushed over by bulldozers to make room for modern housing. But John Wickett, Atherton realtor and amateur historian, came to the rescue. He had it picked up by movers and hauled bodily away. But where to put it? Local building inspectors would not permit him to set it down again—a sub-standard structure, they said, which nobody attempted to deny. So he hauled it, with county permission, to the top of King's Mountain to some property that he owned, and there it stands—uncracked and unscathed by this adventure. It was used temporarily as a radio broadcasting station, and in 1963 it was waiting on its lonely summit for some other opportunity to be useful.

A historic event of preeminent interest to all Californians is the discovery of San Francisco Bay, which took place from a viewpoint in San Mateo County. It is still possible to trace the route of the Portolá Expedition up the Peninsula and to note the camp sites—beginning with Gazos Creek, then San Gregorio Creek where a bronze marker stands by the roadside giving details. Then Purissima Creek and the flea-infested huts of Las Pulgas; next the uncertain camp on Pilarcitos or Frenchman Creek; and finally, the one at Martini's Creek, before the climb up San Pedro Mountain.

Hill-climbing buffs will be rewarded, if the weather is clear, by a climb to the summit of this ridge to view the scene that puzzled Portolá and his men: the beach running north, the turn of the coast to the west, Point Reyes on the distant horizon, the Farallón Islands. Down the hill northward, one may visualize in his imagination the camp by the creek where the Spaniards waited while Ortega scouted the country to the north. Finally, at the north edge of the valley stands a bronze marker where the expedition turned inland to view the "great estuary" from the summit of Sweeney Ridge. It is hoped that some day an adequate memorial or museum atop this ridge will tell the story of this most significant expedition in California history.

A roadside sign on Skyline Boulevard points to the site, now under water, where Portolá camped after crossing the ridge; from there, by just what route one can only imagine, the party reached the spot on San Francisquito Creek by the historic *palo alto*. Under this famous "tall tree" is another marker to tell the story.

There are two more markers of Spanish history. In San Mateo, on Arroyo Court near West Third Avenue, there is a bronze marker to tell that on that creek (*arroyo*) Col. Juan Bautista de Anza camped in 1776 after selecting the sites for the Mission and Presidio of San Francisco. On the same plaque it is recorded that there Moraga and the families that Anza had brought from Mexico to found San Francisco rested for three days before their final day's trip to their destination.

A few steps from this monument, on El Camino Real near Baywood Avenue, is a small plaque placed by the local chapter of the Daughters of the American Revolution, to mark the site of the Mission outpost or Hospice that stood until 1869 as a relic of Franciscan activities down the Peninsula.

## Early American Heritage

A decrepit and weather-beaten farmhouse stood empty on a high spot overlooking the ocean until the Freeway was carved through following the route of the old mission trail to San Pedro Valley. Then, with its surrounding buildings, it was wrecked, and the bulldozers chewed away the hillside until the spot where it had stood could no longer even be identified. And nobody knew or cared that it was once the pioneer home of Michael Comerford.

And who was he? Nobody great or famous, only one of the group of young men who in 1853 bought their small farms from the U. S. Government, built their homes, and planted the virgin land to crops; who saw their friends and neighbors evicted from their similar farms because the Lake Merced Rancho owners claimed the land, and who joined in the long legal battle for their rights.

Such has been the cruel fate of many other one-time neat farmhouses tucked away in sheltering valleys, where lived the Thorntons and other members of the North San Mateo Settlers' Union who made their bit of history; where, along with their colts and calves, the children also grew up, went to school, and in time became adults and went their scattered ways. Now not only are the houses, barns, and fences gone, but even the hills have been pushed into the valleys, and on the flattened plain stand rows and rows of doll-house dwellings on man-shaped land that bears not even a faint resemblance to the once rolling hills of pioneer days.

So the heritage of American beginnings in our area is being obliterated. Only on the Coastside do many early farmhouses remain. Among the most famous are the Johnston houses at Half Moon Bay, and, south of Pescadero, the Cascade Ranch, the Steele places, and the Isaac Graham house. And interested citizens ponder over which, if any, are worth in historic value what it would cost to preserve them.

In assessing these historic values, associations suggested themselves, demanding at least some consideration along with age and architecture. There is the case of General Frederick Steele, West Point graduate and brother of the Pescadero dairymen, who served as a combat officer throughout the Civil War, and came to the Peninsula broken in health, to die soon afterward. In Redwood City the home of General Patrick Edward Connor, another Civil War Veteran, still stands. General Connor, who previously served in the Mexican War, and who is credited later with the killing of Three-Fingered Jack of the "Murietta Gang", commanded California troops in the Civil War. He started a three-year tour of duty in Benicia and ended it in Salt Lake City, guarding Western centers and transit routes against possible seizure by Confederates.

So far, in San Mateo County, the only early-American building acquired by public funds for public preservation and use is Dr. Tripp's Woodside store. Built in 1854, in the early California style of up-and-down board and batten, it is maintained by the County as in part a country store and in part a house museum on the theme of Dr. Tripp and his community.

There are some privately owned collections: The Shine family farmhouse on Cañada Road near Woodside is completely furnished in the style of the late Nineteenth Century, and on the Coastside, south of Pescadero, Mr. Frank Latta is planning to use his large collection of antiques in building a pioneer village and recreation center.

Some historic sites of the American period have at least been marked with plaques. These include the site of the first sawmill, built by Charles Brown on Alambique Creek in Woodside; the site of the village of Searsville which is now partly under the water of Searsville Lake. In down-town Redwood City, a plaque on a store building marks the approximate site where ships were built; on Sandhill Road, east of Searsville, a monument and bronze plaque indicate the area where Dennis Martin's chapel and cemetery were; and in San Mateo, on El Camino Real at Second Avenue, a small plaque designates the adjoining house as (in part) the San Mateo House or stagecoach hotel, later the home of Captain Edward Taylor.

At the northerly edge of the county, near Lake Merced, is the site, marked in 1917 by the Native Sons of the Golden West, where a famous duel was fought; there on September 13, 1859, United States Senator David C. Broderick and David S. Terry, a Justice of the California Supreme Court, met to shoot out their political and personal differences. Broderick's shot went into the ground but Terry took careful aim; Broderick was mortally wounded and died three days later. This affair had the effect of eventually putting an end to dueling in California.

Site marking still goes on. Only as recently as March 2, 1963, the fun-and-history-loving order of E Clampus Vitus dedicated a plaque at the site of the one-time village of Purissima, four miles south of Half Moon Bay, on the banks of Purissima Creek. Here was the large home of Henry Dobbel, together with a big school, stores, a hotel, saloon, boarding houses, and blacksmith shop. The coming of the automobile made all these things unnecessary, and remaining there now are only the town's second school house, now used as a residence, and the cemetery.

Historic buildings and sites, when preserved and marked, become symbols of our cultural heritage. The heritage itself cannot, of course, be pinned down exclusively to any community, nor can it be carved into local fragments, or even precisely defined. But local symbols, preserved and cherished, are like pictures in a book. They can interpret this heritage in a language much clearer and stronger than words.

As we ponder a roadside plaque we can "see" Portola and his saddle-weary Spanish explorers toiling up this very hill; or we can picture right here, on the banks of this creek, men with cant-hooks and crowbars laboriously rolling a log into position to be ripped into planks by a busy upright saw, bobbing up and down on a crank.

Or we contemplate the Woodside Store, filled in its day with everything from horse blankets to bins of sugar and flour. This is local history, in our own community, brought to life for us by the preserved symbols of our cultural heritage.

But the values to be found in local history reach also to another level. We are studying, let us say, the growth and power of the great Spanish Empire in the Americas, which started with Columbus and through a span of two or three centuries dominated most of the Western Hemisphere. How did those Spaniards do it?

For an important part of the answer we have but to look around us, for here in the symbols of our own local history are the footprints of the Spaniards. The mission with its outposts and the presidio for their protection—here is the famous Spanish formula for conquest; the State and the Church, marching hand in hand, to convert and control the natives.

Or perhaps we have read the story of Manifest Destiny—the blind, aggressive faith in an inevitable greatness for American democracy which pushed Yankee enterprise and way-of-life to the Pacific Coast. Here the mementos of our own sawmill men, our road-house merchants, and our squatters, illuminate and clarify the process at its westernmost limit.

In sum, since all history is one, the relics and markers of our own community's early years can open for us windows of understanding, and give us vision to see these local events in their larger meaning: as manifestations *"right here"* of movements covering the world-wide stage of human achievement.

The College of San Mateo's First Home
(Photo taken circa 1915)

HERE FOR ONE YEAR (1922-1923) the College of San Mateo's first students, all thirty of them, were sandwiched in with the high school. In 1927, after four years in the former Kohl mansion, the sturdy "Junior College" returned to this Baldwin Avenue building, filling it now with its student body of 500.

Here it weathered both the Depression and World War II—the former swelling its enrollment to the bursting point because there were no jobs, the latter sapping its manpower, leaving only a skeleton crew to hold the home front. In the booming post-war years the growing College spread into three campuses, and in 1963 came the big move to College Heights.

In this building too, the County Historical Museum was born (1941) in a former classroom. Here it remained and grew, always under the wing of the College, and from here in '63 it joined the trek to the new hill-top campus.

# *Sources*

It has not seemed necessary to encumber this little volume with footnotes and bibliographical data. Reference is made instead to the sources listed in the *History of San Mateo County* published in 1938, and to the archive of information that has been accumulated over a period of some twenty years in our County Historical Museum. For the purposes of this book, these have been supplemented by files of the local and metropolitan newspapers, the records in city halls and the county courthouse, and by personal interviews.

Most of the pictures used are from our own collection at the Musem. Grateful credit for gifts or loans is hereby acknowledged. The first end sheet is by George N. Keyston, and the frontispiece is from the San Francisco Water Department, reproduced and donated by Harry W. Tracy. Page 14, Pedro Evencio, is from Stanford University Library, discovered and donated by Alan K. Brown, and "Indian Joe" is by Dr. Harold F. Taggart; page 22, Anza, is from *Anza's California Expeditions* by H. E. Bolton; page 43, Sanchez, Mrs. Rose Uribe; page 56, mountain logging scene, by Moulin Studios; page 57, sawmill, from Mrs. Fannie Steele; page 58, Redwood City, Library of Congress.

Page 67, San Mateo House, is from the California Historical Society; page 69, toll house, from the A. T. Shine family; page 69, road crew, by California Division of Highways; page 70, ground breaking, T. Louis Chess; page 84, John Greer, Mrs. Joseph Greer; page 92, W. D. M. Howard, Mrs. A. Mitchell-Innes; page 97, train, Mike Burton; page 101, J. C. Flood, and Leland Stanford, both from Wells Fargo Bank History Room; page 102, F. D. Atherton, Society of California Pioneers; page 104, A. Hayward, Wells Fargo Bank History Room; page 110, Mills mansion, Moulin Studios.

Page 117, New Place, is by courtesy of the Burlingame Country Club; page 117, Wm. H. Crocker, Mrs. Helen Potter Russell; page 118, Mrs. Carolan and "The Carolands", San Francisco Examiner; page 124, lighthouse, Moulin Studios; page 132, loading steamer, and page 138, cheese factory, Mrs. Fannie Steele; page 139, R. I. Knapp, F. Hal Higgins; page 139, teachers, Mrs. Mary Azevedo; page 144, airview, Air-Photo Company, Palo Alto; page 154, Menlo Park Gate, Oscar H. Olson, and Camp Fremont, Mrs. Norma Rosenquist; page 166, Stanford University, G. R. Clevenger; page 168, Crystal Springs Dam, page 190, big trees, page 194, Searsville, page 195, San Gregorio Beach, page 197, El Camino Real, and the final end sheet, all from Moulin Studios.

The cover design, the art work on maps, and the drawing on page 169 are by Peter Lo Bianco of the Laguna Salada school district.

Permission to quote has been granted by the following copyright holders: the *Saturday Review* (Arnold Toynbee, page 1, and August Heckscher, page 145); the *Thomas Y. Crowell Company* (Nellie van de Grift Sanchez, page 17, from "A Short History of California" by Hunt and Sanchez); and *William Morrow & Company* (Major Horace Bell, page 35, from "On the Old West Coast").

# Index

212

214